Joe Stahlkuppe

Irish Setters

Everything About Purchase, Care,
Nutrition, Breeding, Behavior, and Training

With illustrations by Michele Earle-Bridges
and 27 Color Photos

Consulting Editor: Matthew M. Vriends, PhD

Photo Credits: Michele Earle-Bridges: pages 45, top, bottom left and right; 63 top left and right, bottom left and right; back cover top right. Gary W. Ellis: inside front cover; pages 10 top, bottom left and right; 27, 28 top, bottom left and right; 64 top left; back cover bottom left. Wim van Vught: front cover; pages 9 top and bottom; 46 top and bottom; 64 top right and bottom; back cover top left, bottom right.

About the Author: Joe Stahlkuppe, who writes a column for a pet industry magazine, is a lifelong dog fancier and breeder. Employed as a regional sales director for a major pet food manufacturer, he is also the author of Barron's *Pomeranians, a Complete Pet Owner's Manual.*

Advice and Warning: This book is concerned with buying, keeping, and raising Irish setters. The publisher and the author think it is important to point out that the advice and information for Irish setter maintenance applies to healthy, normally developed animals. Anyone who buys an adult Irish setter or one from an animal shelter must consider that the animal may have behavioral problems and may, for example, bite without any visible provocation. Such anxiety-biters are dangerous for the owner as well as for the general public.

Caution is further advised in the association of children with an Irish setter, in meetings with other dogs, and in exercising the dog without a leash.

All inquiries should be addressed to:
Barron's Educational Series, Inc.
250 Wireless Boulevard
Hauppauge, New York 11788

Library of Congress Catalog Card No. 91-39168

International Standard Book No. 0-8120-4663-3

Library of Congress Cataloging-in-Publication Data

Stahlkuppe, Joe.
   Irish setters : everything about purchase, care, nutrition, breeding, behavior, and training / Joe Stahlkuppe; with illustrations by Michele Earle-Bridges; consulting editor, Matthew M. Vriends.
     p. cm.
   Includes index.
   ISBN 0-8120-4663-3
   1. Irish setters. I. Title.
SF429.I7S73 1992
636.7'52—dc20   91-39168
                        CIP

PRINTED IN HONG KONG
2345   4900   09876543

Contents

Contents

Foreword

No breed of dog ever has been more blessed by its beauty than the Irish setter, or more cursed. Possessing what is perhaps the most distinctive color in all of the canines, the red setter from Ireland, this rollicking, happy, big dog has been among the most popular breeds in the United States for over a century. This popularity, like its beauty, has not been without a price.

When a breed of dog becomes the object of public adoration, the breed often suffers. When the color of a dog's coat takes precedence over the capabilities of the dog itself, bad times for the breed can be predicted. To be the best of human companions and helpers, a dog, any dog, must be taken as a complete package with attractiveness weighing equally with ability in the final analysis.

When I began this book, I talked with a number of people whose experience with "Irish setters" had not been good. They, their neighbors, or some family member had owned dogs described as "beautiful, but hyperactive without much sense."

With the completion of this book, I must tell each of these people that they have been the victims of a hoax, a sham. The dogs they were describing were not Irish setters at all, for I have found the genuine article, the once and still great red setter from Ireland! The great dogs do exist in red coats and they are everything their record boasts them to be! The other dogs are imposters, merely neurotics in red! The true well-bred, well-trained Irish setter in the hands of a well-prepared owner is that rarest of combinations—beauty *and* ability.

Much appreciation is due to a number of very special people. Thanks and love to my wife Cathie and son Shawn for their ongoing support. I owe much to my friends at Barron's including consulting editor Dr. Matthew Vriends and senior editor Don Reis. Appreciation also goes to Fredric L. Frye, DVM, for his assistance in medical areas. Michele Earle-Bridges, an artist of clear and consistent ability, deserves much praise.

I would like to personally thank the hardworking and often underappreciated staff of the Birmingham, Alabama public library who have watched this book go from an idea to a place on the shelf with the other dog books.

My sincerest regard goes to Irish setter breeders Sheila Smith, Bill Atkins, Connie Vanacore, along with red setter advocate Bob Sprouse and the many others who helped me discover, for myself, the quality and beauty that is the *real* Irish setter. Final appreciation is for three great red dogs: Palmerston, who ironically saved from death would have the profoundest of impacts on the Irish setter breed; Champion Milson O'Boy, perhaps the greatest show dog of all time and who achieved a celebrity status seldom known to human or dog; and the red legend Smada Byrd, who set field trial records that stand to this day!

Joe Stahlkuppe

Understanding the Irish Setter

The first time that a person sees an Irish setter is an experience that never will leave them: a large, nearly flame-colored dog with the regal air of royalty combined with all the mischief and sparkle of a small boy. Irish setters are a breed apart. They never are mistaken for another breed. No other breed has exactly the same color as an Irish setter. Although also a setter like its cousins, the Gordon setter and the English setter, there are marked physical and personality differences in this extended family. (One old Irish setter breeder once remarked that you could shave all the hair off of an English setter, a Gordon setter, and an Irish setter and you could still tell the Irishman—he'd be "the best-lookin' bald dog o' the three!")

Physical beauty for the Irish setter has been a two-edged sword. The dog is so breathtakingly and gloriously stunning that often the attractiveness became an end unto itself. To some, the Irish setter has been allowed to become "just another pretty face." But to the people who really know and love the breed, the Irish setter is a treasure just waiting for the right owner to come along and discover it and turn this mahogany red bundle of energy into something both beautiful and useful. This treasure isn't for everyone, only for those willing to do the mining and the refining to make an Irish setter into that something special it has all the potential to be.

Origin and History of the Breed

Citizens of the Emerald Isle never have been shy or withholding when it comes to discussing the fine qualities of things Irish. But time and the Irish mists have drawn the heather over the precise origins of this one "son of Ireland"—the beautiful and useful Irish setter.

It is fairly certain that the breed was developed and recognized during the eighteenth century. It also seems likely that the big red dogs came from the discriminant blending of the sporting dogs of the time—the spaniels, bloodhounds, pointers, and some infusion of genetic material from the setter cousins,

Gordon and English. Just how this blending took place or precisely where in Ireland is unknown. Dogs at the time were acknowledged and remembered for their working abilities rather than their none-too-carefully-recorded pedigrees.

Three distinct color strains were common in Ireland in earlier times—solid red, red and white, and an interesting red with very small white sprinkles. These three colors were each fostered in different parts of Ireland. Color differences became important to Irish dog breeders with proponents of each color claiming superiority for their color and strain. The solid red (or self-reds as they were called) were objected to as difficult to see and in danger of being shot (a sentiment still heard from some hunters today). Self-red backers countered that their solid-colored dogs were somewhat camouflaged and as such could get nearer to the game birds!

With the advent of dog shows in England in the mid 1800s, the Irish setter began a new chapter in its development. With shows came debate on just what constituted an Irish setter. Although this debate was spirited, eventually compromises were made and standards were set. By 1860, the first dog show to have a separate Irish setter class was held in Birmingham, England. Even so, there continued to be some red and white dogs shown with the self-reds.

In 1870, a dog named Palmerston changed things forever. A hunting dog before he was a show dog, Palmerston (or so the story goes) was once sentenced by his owner, a Mr. Moore, to be destroyed. Not really wanting to kill the dog (and perhaps sensing a chance for a little pocket money), Moore's kennel man sold Palmerston to dog fancier, J. M. Hilliard. Hilliard, although not enthusiastic about Palmerston, began to show him in 1875. Palmerston went on to have a phenomenal show career and an even better career as a stud dog. He repaid Hilliard handsomely by becoming a popular and profitable sire of excellent Irish setters. It seems fitting that Palmerston has been (and is) credited as the most important sire in the development of the modern Irish setter.

Understanding the Irish Setter

American dog enthusiasts and sportsmen became a ready market for Irish red setters. Prices often were steep, but enough quality dogs arrived in the United States to establish a strong and thriving following for the Irish setters in both the show ring and the field.

The field efforts of the Irish setter would one day be superseded by the pointer and the English setter. But Irish setters in the show ring would be another matter. After World War I, there would be a "red explosion," the equal of which rarely has been seen. The Irish setter became "the" dog to own. Early celebrities, like film stars Mary Pickford and Janet Gaynor, owned and promoted their Irish setters. Irish setters were on the move, in the ring if not in the field (although many breeders did try to keep the hunting skills honed on even their best show dogs). Top quality Irish setters began to be produced consistently, and what had begun with a dog with a death sentence over his head became the development of the beautiful and useful Irish setter of today.

The Nature of the Irish Setter

The Irish setter can be accurately classified as a large dog, standing two feet high or more at the shoulder. As setters go, the Irish has more dash and flair than the usually staid English and is perhaps a little more boisterous than the Gordon. The big dog is a bright, fun-loving sort with strong attachments to family and friends. Fans point out that the Irish setter is an excellent babysitter. His size and gentle disposition make him able to withstand the hair pulling, the tugging, and the pokes inflicted by a small child. Irish setters have been known to, without any specific training whatsoever, guide small children away from unsafe situations, placing their considerable bodies between the tot and the danger.

The Irish setter, as beautiful as it may be, is *not* a breed for everyone. Great popularity hurt the Irish setter as a breed, in some fairly subtle ways. Some indiscriminate breeding in the past (when anything that even looked like an Irish setter was bred regard-

The anatomy of the Irish setter:

1. skull	6. loin	13. front pastern
2. ears	7. tail	14. forequarters
3. neck	8. hindquarters	15. brisket
4. shoulder	9. hock	16. chest
5. withers	10. rear pastern	17. muzzle
	11. stifle	18. cheek
	12. ribcage	19. stop

Understanding the Irish Setter

less of physical defects or temperament) left some Irish setters with "hyper" or high strung personalities. These dogs should be only in the hands of skillful, patient owners who have the needed time to spend with this type of dog. Even Irish setters not so affected, generally will be large and rambunctious dogs that may not fit each and every life-style. A well-chosen Irish setter puppy from a well-chosen bloodline or strain with some well-prepared owners can result in an excellent family dog, show dog, obedience dog, or field dog. The accent here is on care in choosing and in preparation.

If one emphasizes good personality and temperament of a strain (or family) and the parentage of a prospective puppy beforehand, then owning an Irish setter can be a true pleasure. This is a loving, gentle, intelligent dog that can be molded into the kind of pet of whom one's grandchildren tell their grandchildren. But the old truism, "You get what you pay for," *never* has been truer than with Irish setters.

An Irish setter from a good genetic background with appropriate and consistent training will make you an excellent companion. If it comes from top-of-the-line show stock, your dog possibly could become a show dog, perhaps even a champion. If from obedience trial or generally intelligent parentage, your Irish setter could earn any of several obedience degrees. If from a field trial or hunting strain, your dog may become a good hunting dog and maybe even a Field Champion within the breed. There are some Irish setters that can do all of these things. But these achievements are not accidental. The days of lucky accidents, as in the case of Palmerston, are over. If you want a specific outcome from your Irish setter you must select for it, plan for it, and train for it. Otherwise, you probably should forget it.

The Irish Setter in the Show Ring

There is no breed of dog in the world that belongs in the show ring more than does the Irish

No breed of dog is more at home in the show ring than is the Irish setter. This has helped and hurt the breed!

setter. It doesn't matter that Irish setters originally were bred to be sporting dogs. In the show quality Irish setter there is a blending of show dog and dog show that few breeds ever equal and none surpass.

For anyone who ever has owned and really cared about a dog of any breed or mixture of breeds, the sight of a well-groomed, well-bred Irish setter on display is truly memorable. The beauty of the Irish setter is never more evident than in the Best-in-Show judging. A gorgeous, stately, joyful Irish setter going up against the best of the best has brought more than one ringside crowd to its feet in thunderous applause. If there was ever a dog truly in its element, the Irish setter in the show ring comes close to it.

Before an Irish setter can become a top show dog, the show quality breeding must be there. Knowl-

Irish setter mothers almost always take excellent care of ▶ their generally sizable litters. The puppies will be nursed for about six weeks.

Understanding the Irish Setter

edgeable, show-oriented care must be there with lots of good food and pure water. Consistent show-centered training must be there. Good show grooming must be there. Sound temperament and a desire to compete and win absolutely must be there. Without all of these indispensable (and a few more) aspects, no Irish setter can hope to be a champion or even a passable show specimen. One Irish setter breeder with a philosophical leaning observed: "There is such magic when you see a really good Irish setter in a really good dog show that you would almost believe that if either had not existed the other would have invented it!" As a point of historical fact, the very *first* dog (of any breed) to win a championship in the United States was Elcho—an Irish setter!

The Irish Setter in Obedience Trials

American Kennel Club obedience trials (a set of tests to determine the ability of a dog to obey certain commands and accomplish certain tasks) have been in existence in the United States since the mid-1930s. The Irish setter is a breed that has shown a particular competence in these trials, which were brought over after great success from England. In what would become one of the fastest-growing canine activities in the United States, the Irish setter fanciers readily grasped obedience trials as a way to showcase their breed's abilities. Many prominent Irish setter kennels have actively participated in and supported dog shows, obedience trials, and field trials.

Since the beginning, countless Irish setters have competed for the obedience trial titles. These titles in order of increasing difficulty are Companion Dog (CD), Companion Dog Excellent (CDX), Util-

Top: Puppies begin to learn pack behavior by playing and roughhousing with each other.
Bottom: At seven weeks of age the youngsters are ready to go their separate ways. Each one will need good care and affection in its new home.

ity Dog (UD), and Utility Dog Tracking (UDT). The top obedience title is the Obedience Trial Champion (the only title that goes *before* the winning dog's name as the others all go *after* the name, that is, Red Rover, CDX). Hundreds upon hundreds of Irish setters have earned obedience trial titles. Some Irish setters have really distinguished themselves in obedience work. The very *first* dog (of any breed) to become a show champion, a field champion, and a UDT was an Irish setter—Dual Champion Red Arrow Show Girl, UDT!

The Irish Setter in the Field

Long before there were dog shows, obedience trials, or field trials, red dogs were helping Irish hunters find and put meat on the table. Beautiful or not, the Irish setter initially was bred to be a hunting dog. It was in this role that the Irish setter first attracted attention. This attention has led to the great popularity that the breed has enjoyed for over a hundred years throughout the world.

Irish setters participated in the very *first* combined field trial and dog show to be held in the United States in Memphis, Tennessee on October 7, 1874, and *won it!* However, in most of this century, as the Irish setter won acclaim in the show ring, pointers and English setters, bred not for the ring but for the field, have dominated the field trials and the field trial championships. Like his cousin, the black and tan Gordon setter, the Irish became known more for his parading down an aisle in a dog show or strolling with its owner on the boulevard than for stealthily seeking out game birds in the hinterlands. To be sure, there always have been Irish setters (some of them even show champions!) that have held up their end of the bargain as good hunting dogs. Some Irish dogs also compete very well in trials within the breed, but the show ring Irish setter has been conspicuously absent from the great field trials, now the almost exclusive province of the field-bred pointers and English setters. (It is also true that there are English pointers and English

11

setters in the show ring, but most of these dogs are also quite different from their field trial-bred namesakes.)

In the early 1950s, a group of field trial enthusiasts dismayed by the absence of Irish setters in general competition began an experiment. Using the best of the, then rare, hunting strain Irish setters combined with the top field trial English setters in the country, Ned LeGrande of Douglasville, Pennsylvania bred the two lines together. He produced what is now known as the red setter, a legitimate contender for field trial honor in the red coat of the old Irish dogs. The red setter is supported by the National Red Setter Field Trial Club of America and registered under the auspices of the American Field Dog Stud Book.

The Irish Setter as a Canine Athlete

Success in the show or obedience ring requires the use of abilities (mental and physical) that are not required of the average backyard dog. Of course a hunting dog or a field trial dog certainly will have to be in better condition than many pet dogs are. Different competitive levels call for different strengths and accented abilities. One factor that cannot be overlooked is the great natural athleticism of the breed. Not only have Irish setters done well in traditionally accepted activities, but they have been drafted into some nontraditional sports as well.

Over the years, the Irish setter has been raced against greyhounds and used to pull carts and perform in a death-defying circus act (complete with big cats!). The Irish setter also became a sled team racer of reknown. In all of these out of breed character activities the Irish setter has done remarkably well.

The Irish Setter as a Companion

It is in the role of pet and companion that the Irish setter can and does make its greatest contribution. The closeness of the early Irish hunter with his dogs made it difficult to keep a dog of uncertain stability or poor temperament. The toughness of the life in those early days also mediated against the overly sensitive or shy dog. Irish setter origins thus brought a sweet and gentle nature into the breed that made it one of the most popular in the United States and the world.

Large, bright, high-energy but slow maturing dogs bring greater responsibilities to their owners. The Irish setter can learn bad habits as easily (or perhaps more easily) as good habits. To own a dog possessed of such grace, beauty, and pure athletic ability and then to have the dog be ruined by a lack of training, a lack of adequate exercise, and a lot of acquired bad habits is a real shame! Generally speaking, the poorly-adjusted Irish setter stems from a poorly-prepared owner.

Not known as a barker, the Irish setter is also not a bully. The size and agility of the red dog generally keeps it from having to prove something to another dog on a chance encounter. But it is still important that the Irish setter *not* be allowed to range freely without human supervision. Such a dog can become a nuisance to others or a potential danger to itself. There is a common view that the people who have the best companion dogs are the best companions to their dogs. This is certainly doubly true of the Irish setter and its owners. The potential is there for most Irish setters to be the finest pets a person could imagine. If that potential is not reached, one cannot blame the dog.

The Pitfalls of Popularity

When a breed gains national acceptance and tremendous popularity, the longtime supporters and fans of the breed cringe. Popularity can do many things for a breed of dogs, many of them bad. Because of the "red explosion," the Irish setter became one of the most popular dogs in the world. The big red dogs are still trying to get over it!

Unscrupulous individuals, seeking to mass-produce as many specimens of a breed as possible, often will breed two dogs together without any regard to their health, temperament, or inheritable defects. The puppies produced in such matings aren't true representatives of their breed. Many of the negatives attributed to the Irish setter stem from these unfortunate pups produced by the uncaring to foist off on the unknowing.

American Kennel Club Standard for the Irish Setter

General Appearance: The Irish setter is an active, aristocratic bird dog, rich red in color, substantial yet elegant in build. Standing over 24 inches (61 cm) tall at the shoulder, the dog has a straight, fine, glossy coat, longer on ears, chest, tail and back of legs. Afield it is a swift-moving hunter; at home, a sweet-natured, trainable companion with a rollicking personality.

Head: Long and lean, its length at least double the width between the ears. The brow is raised, showing a distinct stop midway between the tip of the nose and the well-defined occiput (rear point of skull). Thus the nearly level line from occiput to brow is set a little above, and parallel to, the straight and equal line from eye to nose. The skull is oval when viewed from above or front; very slightly domed when viewed in profile. Beauty of head is emphasized by delicate chiseling along the muzzle, around and below the eyes, and along the cheeks. Muzzle moderately deep, nostrils wide, jaws of

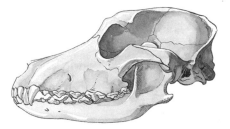

The skull of an Irish setter. Note the length that gives the breed its long and elegant head.

nearly equal length. Upper lips fairly square but not pendulous, the underline of the jaws being almost parallel with the top of the line of the muzzle. The teeth meet in a scissors bite in which the upper incisors fit closely over the lower, or they may meet evenly.

Nose: Black or chocolate.

Eyes: Somewhat almond shaped, of medium size, placed rather well apart; neither deep set nor bulging. Color, dark to medium brown. Expressions soft yet alert.

Ears: Set well back and low, not above level of eye. Leather thin, hanging in a neat fold close to the head, and nearly long enough to reach the nose.

Neck: Moderately long, strong but not thick, and slightly arched; free from throatiness and fitting smoothly into the shoulders.

Body: Sufficiently long to permit a straight and free stride. Shoulder blades long, wide, sloping well back, fairly close together at the top, and joined in front to long upper arms angled to bring the elbows slightly rearward along the brisket. Chest deep, reaching approximately to the elbows; rather narrow in front. Ribs well sprung. Loins of moderate length, muscular, and slightly arched. Topline of body from withers to tail slopes slightly downward without sharp drop at the croup. Hindquarters should be wide and powerful with broad, well-developed thighs.

Legs and Feet: All legs sturdy, with plenty of bone, and strong, nearly straight pasterns. Feet rather small, very firm, toes arched and close. Forelegs straight and sinewy, the elbows moving freely. Hind legs long and muscular from hip to hock, short and nearly perpendicular from hock to ground; well angulated at stifle and hock joints, which like the elbows, incline neither in nor out.

Tail: Strong at root, tapering to fine point, about long enough to reach the hock. Carriage straight or curving slightly forward, nearly level with the back.

Coat: Short and fine on head, forelegs, and tips of ears; on all other parts, of moderate length and flat. Feathering long and silky on ears; on back of

Understanding the Irish Setter

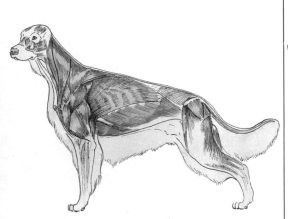

An impressive and utilitarian muscle structure is the basis for the Irish setter's reputation as a versatile canine athlete.

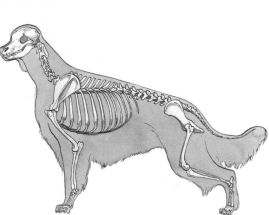

A strongly-built skeleton, dominated by a large ribcage, shows that the Irish setter is a dog built for activity—and *lots* of it!

forelegs and thighs long and fine, with a pleasing fringe of hair on belly and brisket extending onto the chest. Feet well feathered between the toes. Fringe on tail moderately long and tapering. All coat and feathering as straight and free as possible from curl or wave.

Color: Mahogany or rich chestnut red, with no trace of black. A small amount of white on chest, throat, or toes, or a narrow centered streak on skull is not to be penalized.

Size: There is no disqualification as to size. The make and fit of all parts and their overall balance in the animal are rated more important. Twenty-seven inches (69 cm) at the withers and a show weight of about 70 pounds (32 kg) is considered ideal for a dog; the bitch 25 inches (64 cm), 60 pounds (27 kg). Variance beyond an inch up or down to be discouraged.

Gait: In a trot the gait is big, very lively, graceful, and efficient. The head is held high. The hindquarters drive smoothly and with great power. The forelegs reach well ahead as if to pull in the ground, without giving the appearance of a hackney gait. The dog runs as it stands: straight. Seen from the front or rear, the forelegs, as well as the hind legs below the hock joint, move perpendicularly to the ground, with some tendency toward a single track as speed increases. But a crossing or weaving of the legs, front or back, is objectionable.

Balance: At its best, the lines of the Irish setter so satisfy in overall balance that artists have termed it the most beautiful of all dogs. The correct specimen always exhibits balance whether standing or in motion. Each part of the dog flows and fits smoothly into its neighboring parts without calling attention to itself.

Considerations Before You Buy

Is the Irish Setter the Right Dog for You?

Sadly, the Irish setter suffers somewhat from the perceptions of others. Some people see only the finished product without considering what efforts were required to produce that particular show, obedience, or hunting dog. Others insert themselves into a mental picture that usually includes the Irish setter at their feet before a roaring fire in the hearth. Still others visualize how striking they'll be as they walk a gorgeous Irish setter down some street or across a city park. Mental pictures can be created in a fraction of an instant; the real dogs they portray will take years to produce and develop.

Your task is to decide which sort of Irish setter admirer you are. Do you want to work to help develop an Irish setter into a wonderful companion or will your real dog always come in second best to your dream dog?

Before you realistically can decide if an Irish setter is the right dog for you, you must decide if you (and your family) will be the right humans for the Irish setter! There are many responsibilities that go with the many possibilities open to the Irish setter. In order to mold a raw pup into a magnificent adult dog, you will need to recognize several things about the Irish setter *before* you seriously consider ownership:
• Finding a quality Irish setter will take time, money, effort, and perhaps some luck.
• Although Irish setters are bright, intelligent dogs, they mature slowly. When some breeds are already adults by ten or twelve months, it probably will take two full years for your Irish pup to physically grow up. Just because the Irish setter is not a rapid developer doesn't mean that it won't figure out ways to get what it wants (much like a young child will).
• Like any big dog in the home, an Irish setter puppy can wreak havoc in a household unprepared for the active, curious nature of an as-yet-undisciplined young dog. Any large, friendly puppy could possibly knock down a very small child or a senior citizen. A puppy will not know its own strength and in its enthusiasm to make friends actually will frighten those not familiar with dogs.
• It behooves any potential Irish setter owner to make a real effort to obtain the best possible specimen and give it the best possible care and training. Such efforts will go a long way in assuring the best possible dog.

Before you buy an Irish setter, you and each member of your family should be absolutely certain that you want to assume full-time responsibility for this dog. You can reasonably assume that the Irish setter puppy you could purchase next week will still be a member of your family into the twenty-first century! Your Irish setter will be totally dependent on you for every aspect of its care: food, water, companionship, training, housing, and medical attention. If you and the members of your household are not willing or not able to make this type of commitment, perhaps now it *not* the best time for an Irish setter.

The following questions (and others that you can come up with yourself) should be considered before you go any further into buying an Irish setter:
• Is this Irish setter a well-thought-through project rather than just an impulsive, spur-of-the-moment idea?
• Does each person in your household know what having an Irish setter in your home will mean and involve?
• Does each family member want to accept the responsibility for an Irish setter?
• Is each family member willing to give an Irish setter the personal attention that it will need and deserve?
• Does your family have the resources and space that a large dog like an Irish setter will require? (Hopefully a fenced-in yard or access to a good exercise area; at least an hour a day for attention, training, and so on; approximately $50 per month for quality food, regular veterinary care, and equipment.)

• Does your family realize the amount of effort required to just learn about, find, and obtain a top quality Irish setter?

• Does your family recognize the work that will go into training an Irish setter, in order for your dog to be the best possible pet it can be?

These questions may seem to be obvious or even unnecessary, but failure to understand and deal with these areas of concern could result in quite an unpleasant experience for you, your family, and an innocent Irish setter.

A healthy, well-bred, well-cared for, and well-trained Irish setter not only is a beautiful family pet, but a wonderful companion dog. It is also vital that you and your family are equally good dog companions.

The key question must be, "Is the Irish setter the right dog for you?" If the answer is "No," you are to be congratulated for carefully weighing all the factors, and deciding that the big, red Irish dog isn't for you. Your answer may be "Now is not the time to get an Irish setter." You have done the right thing in evaluating your current situation and finding that an Irish setter would not get the things it needs in your current life-style, economic circumstances, lack of time or space.

If your answer, after careful consideration of all the variables and important factors surrounding Irish setter ownership, is "Yes," congratulations! You are about to embark on a most interesting and fun part of your life as you add this new redhead to your family. You can now begin to make some decisions about the age, sex, and background of the Irish setter you will have as a loving friend and family member for the next 10 to 15 years.

A Puppy or an Older Dog?

If you are a novice dog owner and want to pursue the show ring, obedience trials, or field work, you probably would do well with a puppy. Either a puppy or an older dog will do well for companion-ship, but a puppy can grow up with you and also be a devoted pet.

With an older dog, there may be reasons that caused the dog not to work out at its previous home. You would have to be lucky to find an adult Irish setter with the temperament, training, and adaptability to totally fit your needs as well as a home-grown puppy would. That certainly does not mean that there aren't excellent adult Irish setters available from time to time (especially through the Irish Setter Club of America or your local kennel club). Sometimes quality Irish setters are available due to some unforeseen situation; a transfer, an illness, or death in the family can change circumstances that will require finding a new home for the family pet.

Unfortunately for the good adults that are available, there are usually many more not-so-good adults around. You are looking to add a family member, not a whole new set of pre-established problems. If a good Irish setter adult is what you are seeking, you might follow these steps:

• Contact the American Kennel Club or the Irish Setter Club of America (see Useful Addresses and Literature). Tell them of your desire to give a healthy, well-mannered Irish setter the best possible home.

• Contact Irish setter breeders in your area. Let them know who you are and why you could be a good owner for a preconditioned Irish setter.

• Although possible but of lesser reliability, look through the classified ads in your paper. In this case, you need to really research the adult Irish setters offered in this manner very carefully. One thing you will need to remember in any interest area including dogs is "buyer beware."

• A veterinarian or a quality pet store may have or hear of an adult Irish setter in need of a good home.

All Irish setter puppies tend to be adorable. With their big eyes and feet, they can steal your heart immediately. But that's not what you want to have happen. Just because a puppy is appealing at seven or eight weeks of age doesn't mean it is *the* Irish setter for you! You need to spend *at least* as much

Considerations Before You Buy

time and energy in finding the best possible puppy as you would in buying a car (or, as some Irish setter breeders say, in buying a house!).

If you will continually remember that the puppy you choose is going to be with you for the next 10 to 15 years, you'll have the right attitude to withstand the pressures of a cute puppy. If you pick the first Irish setter puppy that you see, you may get the ideal family member you are seeking, but then again you may not!

Someone in the family must be responsible for helping the young puppy become adjusted to its new home. This will be quite a job that should be done before other activities are undertaken. It is important that this key individual want to do the job and is able to do it. It is better to understand right from the start that many children will beg and plead for a puppy promising to take care of it and then forgetting about it within a few days or a week. Your Irish setter puppy deserves better treatment than that. It didn't ask to be brought into your home or into your lives, you made that decision.

A puppy will need to have consistent, high priority care without fail. It is good to remember the example set by cavalrymen in the Old West. No matter how long the day's ride or how hard the day's work, no self-respecting horse soldier would eat or sleep until he had looked to the needs of his horse. This is the same kind of treatment that a young Irish setter will require of you.

An older setter, especially a dog that can adapt readily to its new surroundings, may not need nearly as much care as a puppy. But, an adult still will need time to learn its new role in its new home. If this dog was mistreated anywhere along the line prior to coming to you, it may have a whole set of problems that, even though you treat it well, may linger in the dog's mind. It may have been very close to someone in its old environment and need time to find a new attachment with you or with some member of your family. If you are determined to bring an older Irish setter into your family, in most cases good consistent care will help things work out

for both of you. If some deep-seated problem does exist, a professional trainer or a veterinarian can help you deal with it.

Puppy or adult, you already have begun your apprenticeship as an Irish setter owner. Continue to go to dog shows, obedience trials, or hunting events. Talk with as many Irish setter people as you can. You'll find most of them to be more than willing to share their knowledge with you. Read all you can about Irish setters in particular and dog care in general. Veterinarians, dog groomers, pet store owners, and trainers will have useful ideas and information for you. The opportunity is yours, to learn as much as you can about the breed you really like and then to apply what you've learned to help you obtain, care for, and develop the best possible Irish setter.

Male or Female?

Either sex of the Irish setter can be an excellent choice for you, if you really have decided on what you want in a dog. Irish setter males, in spite of their great beauty, are still male dogs. The female Irish setter, although maybe a slight bit smaller, is still friendly, active, and generally possessing marked devotion to her family. Males will need a little more exercise than will most females. Females bring a different set of problems when they come "in season." The sex of your dog, therefore, comes down to personal preference *or* the sex of the best available puppy. (Note: Unless you have *serious* ambitions to be a dog breeder, don't pass up an exceptional puppy solely on the basis of its sex. For a family pet and companion, both sexes do very well.)

One important concern for you regardless of whether you get a male or a female Irish setter is neutering and spaying. Other than for breeding or the show ring, neutering and spaying will not keep your setter from being able to participate in obedience or field work. Both will be better pets (females won't have the in season problems, males won't

Considerations Before You Buy

have the pursuit of the female in season problems) and you will be able to avoid contributing to an already huge oversupply of puppies awaiting homes.

Males are just that, males, and unless they are constrained can roam throughout a neighborhood when they know a female is in heat. This not only causes your dog to be a nuisance in the neighborhood (opening you to potential legal liability), but also can endanger the life of your dog. Unless there are excellent breeding reasons, neutering your male Irish setter is advisable. (Note: It is unfortunately true that many people seem to feel that neutering their dog is a terrible thing to do to it. In reality, nothing could be further from the truth. Aside from the obvious reasons for spaying a female Irish setter of nonbreeder potential, there are health reasons. Spaying a bitch greatly cuts down on the possibility of breast tumors and certain other medical problems.)

If, however, after most careful consideration, breeding is your considered choice of roles for your Irish setter, you might consider obtaining the absolutely, positively best female puppy available. (This should be a fairly sizable investment.) Treat her with the best of care and training. Depend on the expertise and advice of Irish setter breeders of long experience. You will want to consider breeding her to the best possible male whose pedigree is compatible to hers. Your goal here is to improve the breed. Any health or temperament problems in either the male or female can be passed on to the offspring in the same fashion. Unless you are *seriously* interested in breeding Irish setters with all of the money, time, and effort it will entail, forget it. Casually allowing a litter of puppies to be born is clearly irresponsible on a dog owner's part.

If you do get a male puppy, the chances, in even a show-quality litter at show-quality prices, of your getting a male that will be good enough to use as a stud dog are in the true long shot category. (There are serious, longtime Irish setter breeders who have *never* produced such a puppy in all their years of earnest and informed trying.)

For a pet, either a male or female Irish setter will do as long as it comes from healthy, temperamentally-sound stock. As such, this Irish setter will be able to give you years of great companionship and adoring love. Do your homework, check out the backgrounds of each serious contender to be your Irish setter, and then choose, based on which puppy, male or female, you like best. You will likely get a great pup, either way.

Pet Quality or Show Quality?

There is a great deal of misinterpretation in some breeds in the phrase pet quality. The Irish setter can be one of those breeds. Harking back to the previously mentioned places where indiscriminate breeding of "Irish setters" was conducted, pet quality can be and often is a complete misnomer. From the wrong source you could get a dog that would be a poor pet and have no quality at all!

Knowing what you want from your Irish setter is the best way to deal with this question. "Seek sheep from a shepherd and chickens in the hen house" is an old adage that may help you in your search for an Irish setter. If you want a bird dog or a field trial dog, go to an Irish setter breeder who specializes in Irish setters that are bird dogs or field trial dogs. If you want an obedience dog, buy a puppy from someone who has had success in that area (success preferably with the parents of the puppy you wish to buy!). Dog show enthusiasts (whose Irish setters win regularly in the larger dog shows) are the best place to seek a potential show pup. Potential is the operative word here as it is impossible to predict that any puppy from any litter from any kennel will be a surefire winner.

There will be a number of sources for your Irish setter puppy, but first you must know what you really want. After you know, you should look in the places where that kind of puppy may be most commonly found. Remember, it is far better to get a pet-quality puppy (rejected for some minor conformation or cosmetic flaw) from an outstanding litter than to get the very best pick-of-the-litter from an inferior source.

How to Select an Irish Setter Puppy

You now have more of an idea of what you want: a puppy or an adult, a male or a female, a pet-quality over a show-quality, or an obedience- or a field-trial Irish setter. Before you begin the process that will ultimately lead you to choosing a puppy, there are several things that you can do to make the search easier.

Prepare yourself (and your family) by reading as much as you can about the Irish setter. The public library or a pet store may have some of the books you need. You should contact the Irish Setter Club of America (see Useful Addresses and Literature) for information and contacts with breeders that this national breed club can provide.

Visit as many dog shows as you can (especially those that are held in conjunction with obedience trials). See Irish setters not only in the ring but also in the waiting and grooming areas. Observe the qualities that are important in an Irish setter in these environments (patience, tractability, calmness, and so forth).

You should realistically assess your current living situation. Will you have a fenced-in yard for your Irish setter with a fence of sufficient height to keep an athletic dog at home? If you do not have such a yard, what are the other possibilities for the exercise that an active Irish setter must have in abundance? (You have, of course, realized the folly of letting an Irish setter roam freely.) Many of the negatives attributed to the Irish setters can be traced to inadequate exercise.

You also should take a clear look at your budget. Can you really afford a good quality Irish setter, as well as the other expenses (food, shelter, regular medical care, and so on) that owning such a dog will necessitate?

On the subject of finances, avoid bargain basement Irish setters! You may find what others have discovered—that *the most expensive pet they've ever had was a cheap or even free one!* Of course, there are exceptions to this, but in Irish setters, as in life, "there ain't no free lunch." A number of professional dog breeders related that they could easily afford to give away a pet-quality puppy to an apparently deserving home, but that they rarely did so. As one breeder explained, "When you give some people a dog (or anything else) you seem to devalue the quality or even the spirit of the gift. People simply don't tend to appreciate or give adequate care to a puppy or adult dog that didn't cost them anything to get. No dog deserves that."

Another ironic note about Irish setters is the strange fact that the "inexpensive," pet-quality puppy may be, in the long run, far more costly than some genuine show-potential pups might have been. Genetic or preexisting medical problems can run the price tag on a $100 bargain to well over $1,000 in no time at all. It may be much simpler (and cheaper) to buy an Irish setter puppy from the most outstanding kennel in the country paying whatever that kennel asks for a puppy of the quality you are seeking than to buy one cheaply from your cousin's friend's next-door neighbor.

Finding an Irish setter puppy with show potential will require work on your part. If you are new to purebred dogs, or even if you are not, always let the "buyer beware" motto be your watchword. It is not that finding and acquiring a puppy from show stock is so difficult. It isn't. There are many ethical Irish setter breeders in every section of the United States. The problem comes when you try to fit your goals and aspirations of an awesome show ring dominator onto the ungainly body of an eight-week-old Irish setter puppy. Even the most ethical professional individual, striving to provide you with the best possible puppy, cannot guarantee the ultimate show-worthiness of the adult dog that puppy will become. There are simply too many variables, environmental and otherwise.

Considerations Before You Buy

Irish setter breeders who are members of the Irish Setter Club of America will be the best (and least risky) source for your potential show puppy.

Although there may be good puppies available from a reputable pet store or from the local person whose pet bitch had puppies, you always should try to observe the parents of such a litter. If they are happy, healthy, well-adjusted representatives of the breed (and you are seeking just a pet), you may not do badly. Insist on the same guarantees, paperwork, and medical clearances that you could get as a matter of course from a top-of-the-line breeder. If the local source can't (or won't) supply these items, simply *don't buy the puppy!* Some other factors to watch for are the cleanliness of the premises and the number of dogs kept there.

All reasonable care taken before you purchase a puppy will pay many dividends over the years with a healthy and happy dog. Don't be afraid to ask questions and expect clear answers that can be substantiated. Also don't allow yourself or members of your family to let a cute puppy lure you into making a purchase when you know that you shouldn't. Remember the goals you set for your Irish setter puppy and eliminate any and all that don't fit, regardless of how appealing the puppies may be or how low the price. Don't end up with a new puppy just because it was there and so were you and your checkbook!

Prior to actually selecting a puppy from any source, make certain that the puppy you may buy has these vital documents:

• current health records for the prospective puppy with the dates of all vaccinations, dates when the puppy has been dewormed, and any other treatments it may have received;
• a pedigree (which probably will be only as reliable as the source you have chosen for your puppy) that shows the puppy's line or parentage. A *bona fide* pedigree showing numerous champions, field champions, or obedience title holders may be illuminating as to the basic genetic potential of your puppy;

• the AKC (American Kennel Club) Registration certificate stating that this Irish setter puppy is a purebred with its mother (dam) and father (sire) both being registered Irish setters. You also should receive application forms to forward to the AKC in order to register the puppy in your name; and
• additionally, you will want documentation that the parents are free from certain genetically transmitted defects or conditions, such as HD (Hip Dysplasia, see page 57) or PRA (Progressive Retinal Atrophy, see page 58). These, and other, medical problems can cause you tremendous heartache and expense (not to mention the physical pain that the puppy ultimately may experience.)

If you can't get these documents, *don't buy the puppy!* The world is filled with dog owners who lament that the "breeder never sent the papers!" If you don't pay for the puppy until the necessary papers are in your hand, you'll not have that worry. This is not meant to imply that dog breeders are dishonest, but a very small number are. You should treat these documents as a part of the puppy and you wouldn't want an incomplete puppy, would you?

Most reputable sources also will supply a health and temperament guarantee for any dogs they sell. This is best to have in writing and usually will cover the dog's inherited health and temperament for life. Value those who are so sure of their stock that such a guarantee is their normal way of doing business.

Responsible breeders may have some agreements for you to sign as well. Many breeders take the puppies they sell as a lifetime responsibility and may request some things by which you, the buyer, must abide:
• One such buyer-related item may be a spay or neuter agreement that will keep someone from breeding an obvious pet-quality puppy. This is a reasonable way that a breeder can keep an otherwise fine pet from passing on conformation defects to ill-conceived offspring. (Some breeders make a practice of withholding the registration papers until the buyer returns with a veterinarian's affidavit stating that the puppy has been spayed or neutered.)

• Other breeders will want to impress on you that they retain a strong proprietorial interest in the puppy. If you cannot keep the Irish setter, the breeder may want it returned rather than seeing it passed into other hands or sent to an animal shelter. (Any breeder who makes you commit in such ways as these is probably a very good source for a puppy.)

Hopefully you will have a number of good puppies to choose from if you are willing to be patient. Good Irish setter puppies are never a glut on the market. You may find that you will locate the very breeder you believe will have the kind of puppy you want and have to go on a waiting list (usually with a deposit to hold a puppy). This is a very positive sign for Irish setters as a breed. Quality puppies are always worth waiting for! (It does help a little that Irish setters tend to have large litters!)

When the time does come to choose a puppy, and you have found just the right source of just the right kind of Irish setter strain, you will be prepared. Observe the puppies for some length of time. Pick out that puppy who shows interest in its surroundings, sees you and does not fear you, and which seems to be well-adjusted within the litter itself. Carefully handle each prospective puppy of the litter, paying attention to the one that you already have observed as alert, unafraid, and well adjusted. After handling each puppy, if this pup still ranks high in your estimation, ask the owner what she or he thinks about that pup. Take your time in this process. By now the owner knows the litter well and what you are seeking. You may find exactly the puppy you want, but don't emotionally decide (or allow your family to decide) on any puppy until *your* veterinarian has a look at it. Once the veterinarian says the puppy is sound and healthy, you probably have found your new canine family member.

How to Pick up a Puppy

When picking up a gangly, squirming Irish setter puppy, always support the back end with one hand. With the other hand, hold under the chest for comfort. In this manner, you can look the puppy over without danger of it falling from your hands.

The Irish Setter and the Small Child

The Irish setter is a wonderful dog for children. Many accounts of the sweet natured, red dog caring for even very small children fill to overflowing the oral and written history of the breed. A special relationship or bond seems to develop quickly between an Irish setter and children, especially children in its own family. Although rough play with a very young puppy should be discouraged, most Irish setter pups can stand up to the fierce hugs, tugging, and pulling of little children. Because of the relatively slow maturational process in the Irish setter, it tends to be able to adjust very well to the needs of its young human playmates.

When picking up a puppy, always support its rear and its hind legs with one hand while steadying its chest with the other.

The Irish setter is a great dog with children. As with the active child, the Irish setter needs a great deal of daily exercise.

Aside from the obvious opportunities a child will have as a playmate, the Irish setter can serve as an excellent learning opportunity for any youngster. Although primary care of a young puppy should only be entrusted to someone with the maturity and ability to carry out the job, much can be learned by a child in feeding, watering, and taking care of an Irish setter. Because of the great versatility of the Irish setters, a child's interest can be channeled in several directions—hunting, dog shows, obedience work, and others.

If your children are taught to love and be kind to their Irish setter, you have set the stage for a fantastic chance for them to learn responsibility, loyalty, and dog care. The setter will be their large, red friend who can be trusted to protect them from harm while not posing a danger to other playmates as some guard breeds may.

Irish Setters and Other Pets

As a hunter, the Irish setter is alert and aware of other animals. Common sense will tell you that some adult dogs brought into a family situation where other pets exist may have to adjust. In most cases, it will not take the setter long to learn that the other dogs, cats, and so forth are also family members.

One Irish setter breeder related several stories about her adopting other animals: kittens, rabbits, and the like. Perhaps the greatest example of Irish setter gentleness is an incident where one young male, not much more than a big puppy himself, brought his mistress a fully feathered, unharmed baby blue jay. The little bird had fallen out of its nest and was brought special delivery to her in the young dog's mouth without so much as a feather ruffled. Others have told of their Irish setters carrying turtles, frogs, and even unbroken eggs in their mouths. Although some dogs may learn bad habits relating to other animals, a well-schooled Irish setter is capable of great gentleness.

(Author's note: When my wife was a small child, she and her family had an Irish setter: "Rusty, a big male, would seek out where the family cat had put her kittens and bring several at a time in his large

Among the most beautiful of dogs, the Irish setter has excelled in the show ring, in obedience work, in the field, and as a spirited pet.

22

Considerations Before You Buy

mouth to his special place on the front walk. Plopping down on his stomach, the big dog would gently place the kittens in an enclosure made by his front legs crossed in front of him. He would lick and play with the kittens for about ten minutes and then gather them back into his cavernous mouth and return them to their mother's nest.")

Other dogs in a family or in a neighborhood should have little to fear from an Irish setter. Not known as a bully, nevertheless the full-grown Irish setter has the size and ability to protect himself and his family. Of course, Irish setters should never be allowed to free range as its follow-its-nose mentality could get it into trouble. Unless you are actually with your Irish setter, a fenced-in yard is the best way to keep your red friend out of mishap and potential danger.

The Cost of Keeping an Irish Setter

Initially, you can expect to pay anywhere from $350 to $450 for a pet-quality Irish setter. In some areas and under some circumstances you could pay a little less, but don't count on it. Question any Irish setter puppy that is much below these figures (show-quality pups with potential may cost as much as $500 to $850 or more).

As a larger dog, the Irish setter will need a premium quality dog food. Pay attention to nutrition if you want the best for (and out of) your developing Irish setter. A quality diet will require more of a financial investment, but ultimately will pay off with a healthy, long-lived pet.

Regular veterinary visits will help keep your red dog "in the pink." You should have a regular veterinarian who will know your dog and share your interest in its ongoing care. Your Irish setter probably will need continuing medication as a heartworm preventative in many parts of the United States.

Incidental expenses like leads, collars, flea and tick remedies, and toys always will be necessary. Your Irish setter will not be without cost, either initially or throughout its life. Even if you do *not* intend to involve your dog in showing, obedience trials, hunting, or field trials, you should budget about $50 per month. Of course, this will be a little low in some parts of the country and a little high in others, but this amount should be a good starting point.

Christmas Puppies

Another of the mental pictures that can plague a breed is the apparently innocent, especially heartwarming scene on Christmas morning when you surprise a child with a puppy. The child is, of course, overjoyed and the puppy is probably overwhelmed.

Regardless of how heartwarming this may appear, this mental picture is *not* a good one. Bringing a new puppy into the happy chaos that is called Christmas morning is both unfair and unwise. Such a puppy will be even more bewildered than usual by all the festivities. Unless it is the *only* gift you give your child, the puppy will have to share the spotlight with all the other presents.

Wait a few weeks after Christmas (or even give the puppy several weeks before Christmas) and give the young Irish setter a chance to adjust to your family during normal times. A puppy will need to be the center of attention with appropriate care and amply demonstrated love to get off to the best possible start. Don't ask an eight-week-old Irish setter to compete against anything, especially against one of the busiest holidays of the year! (One breeder of Irish setters had a novel approach that would still allow for a package under the tree when she sold an after-Christmas puppy. She would provide the potential puppy owner with a videotape of useful information about the breed and its care. Tagged to the end of the videotape was a personal message using the names of the children of the family and showing a litter of Irish setter puppies. This creative breeder would explain that one of these puppies would be coming to the children's home, after Christmas!)

23

Caring for Your Irish Setter

Before You Bring Your Irish Setter Home

Whether your Irish setter is a puppy or an adult, a male or a female, a show specimen or a pet-quality dog, a new home will be a stressful circumstance. To alleviate some of this stress and to help your setter get off to the best possible start, there are a number of things you can do to make the move to a new home less of a trauma to your new dog or puppy.

Locate a good pet supply store that has a good stock of equipment and pet food, and employees who have a lot of experience in helping new dog owners get the things they will need. Experienced, helpful sources of information will be invaluable to you especially if this is your first dog.

Based on recommendations from the breeder where you got the Irish setter and from your friends at the pet supply store, purchase the following items.

Buy a sturdy, flat-bottomed bowl for water and another one for food. These should be large enough to be used by your Irish setter for some years to come. The flat-bottomed or broad-based design is to make them more difficult to turn over.

A nonskid placemat on which to put these dishes would be a help in keeping the surrounding floor clean.

Purchase *exactly* the same food the dog has been eating. Change diets, if you must, at some later time when the transition is not so traumatic.

If your setter is to be housebroken, even if it will spend much time in your fenced-in yard with a good doghouse, you will need a large dog carrier (also called a crate or a cage). *This will be your absolutely best investment* after a quality dog food and the dog itself! This cage/crate/carrier also will be your Irish setter's special place within your home.

Again utilizing the breeder's recommendations and with the pet store's help, purchase a lead (sometimes called a leash) and a collar of a size appropriate for your dog or puppy. This collar will be your Irish setter's regular collar (not the training collar suggested in the chapter on training). You should use this permanent collar as a place to attach any license or rabies inoculation tags often required by law. Another good idea is to have a tag made with your name and address in case your Irish setter gets lost or is stolen.

Based on the breeder's or store's suggestions, purchase a good grooming comb and brush. Even while your Irish setter is still a puppy, early brushing will serve as a good way to help the puppy stay neat and also learn appropriate times not to be so boisterous.

Toys will be available at the pet supply store. Irish setters are active and some of this energy can be re-channeled into playing with a sturdy toy.

Outside housing for your Irish setter can be a good idea. Even if you plan to have your new pet share your home with you and your family, an outside shelter and enclosed exercise area will be good to have. For those times when you are not at home, your adult Irish setter will be happier outside. The best type of outside shelter will be determined, in part, by the climate where you live. Discuss this with an area breeder or the pet store.

The Irish setter that spends even part of its time outside without human supervision needs a covered run or a fenced yard.

Caring for Your Irish Setter

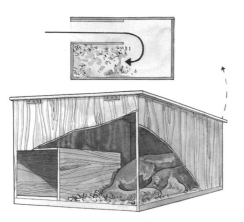

A well-constructed outdoor doghouse will provide a dog with protection from rain, snow, chilling winds, or too much sunshine.

Housebreaking your Irish setter puppy and helping it become a responsible indoor and outdoor canine citizen will make the puppy all the more a member of your family. Although your Irish setter always will need the opportunities that a fenced-in yard can afford, as a people-oriented dog, it also will gain greatly from being able to live with you in your home.

Before you bring your Irish setter puppy into your home, you should puppy-proof all areas to which the puppy will have access. In much the same way that you would prepare a room for a toddler, you will need to remove any items that might cause harm to your inquisitive puppy.

In all the places that the puppy can get to, remove from reach any electrical cords that, upon being chewed by a teething puppy, might cause its death by electrical shock. Also put out of the pup's reach any toxic plants (call your veterinarian, garden center, or extension service for a list of possible poisonous house and yard plants). Search for and pick up any tacks, pins, beads, or any other items that might be swallowed by a young pup and do it

harm. Check for exposed woodwork (especially in older homes) that may have been painted with a lead-based paint that could poison a gnawing puppy. Also be certain that the woodwork and any furniture in reach hasn't been treated with some toxic chemical polish or spray. Remove any heavy items that possibly could be pulled off or fall on and cause injury or death to your puppy. This includes hot pots and pans as the puppy grows taller and able to reach the stove top.

Close off any balconies or porches that may have railings or ironwork that could trap a puppy's head. Also protect your Irish setter from any residual poisons left behind by the exterminator for vermin (rats, mice, roaches).

Your home will be a whole new experience to an Irish setter puppy whose entire previous life was limited to a whelping box and pen with its mother and littermates. You must now be certain that this inexperienced young dog isn't injured in its new environment.

Stairs are another possible danger area. Although an Irish setter is a sturdy puppy, a fall down a flight of steps or off a landing can do a lot of damage. Close off any unsafe areas, or any areas you will want to make out-of-bounds. Remember that an Irish setter is a breed that has a well-developed sense of smell. A young puppy following its curious nose could get stuck in places that you could never imagine.

Remind your family members of the new responsibilities they will have with a puppy literally underfoot. Doors must be closed carefully to avoid catching a following puppy. Doors also must be watched when open to keep the puppy from bounding heedlessly into a crowded street or into other equally dangerous mischief. Doggy gates (like the gates that protect small children) should restrict your puppy in its early days from going where you do not wish it to go. If your puppy has access to your garage or driveway, any movement of the car in or out must be preceded by a safety check to make certain that the puppy is not in harm's way.

You should arrange to bring your puppy home at a time when you can have several days to help the youngster get settled in. Adjustment to a new home is always traumatic, but your patience and the loving exuberance of your new Irish setter will make everything all right.

Bringing Your Irish Setter Puppy Home

You have chosen the best possible Irish setter you could find, based on your careful assessment of the things you want in this new red-headed family member. You have designated a good, safe exercise area (a fenced-in yard is ideal). You may have decided to have an outside shelter for those times when you will not be home (after your Irish setter is over the first few weeks of new home adjustments). You have puppy-proofed the inside areas where your puppy will be. You have obtained the recommended items and you are now ready to bring your new responsibility home.

In the often confusing days of adjusting to its new environment, your pup will need the comforting "sameness" of its crate or den. You will see the den as an excellent way to regulate your active dog's inside activities and as a training tool in housebreaking.

For a young, eight- or nine-week-old puppy the trip home itself may be both interesting and frightening. If possible, have that family member who will have primary responsibility hold the pup as you ride home (of course, if the trip is several hours in length, use the carrier). Never let the unsteady puppy ride unsupported in the car with you; the risk of accidents or injuries is too great.

You probably will want to have the responsible family member wear an old robe and have some towels handy, because motion sickness is quite possible in a young puppy. If the journey is a long one, stop often for exercise and "nature" breaks and to reassure the puppy.

Upon arriving at your home, first take the Irish setter pup to that specially chosen area where it will be expected to defecate and urinate. Wait there with the pup. If the area is not a fenced-in yard, this is a good time to break out the new collar and lead. Let the pup nose around. One smart Irish setter breeder always bags up a little of the paper or even waste material from the pup's first home for the new owners to use to "prime the pump." Place this in the chosen spot, and when your pup does eliminate there, praise it lavishly. Whatever you do, *never* correct or punish the puppy at this location! Such actions only will confuse it. Praise is the order of the day. With this first relief session, your dog's training has just begun. Your Irish setter puppy will want to please you. It won't take the puppy long to associate the special outside location with relieving itself and the loving praise from the new human. Following this method of praise combined with consistency, you will have little trouble helping your puppy get off to a good start.

When you take the puppy back inside, always observe it and be ready to dash for the door with a puppy who needs "to go." Thus, by gently getting its attention, you will reinforce the idea that the spot outside is where it defecates or urinates. Use of the den also comes into focus here. When the new puppy gets tired of playing and checking things out, put it into its den/crate. The pup will soon learn where it is to sleep (a lesson you will be grateful you can get across quickly). Often a tired Irish setter puppy will go to the den on its own. Remember that puppies, like human babies, spend a lot of their early days and weeks sleeping. Having its den nearby will help teach your puppy that the crate is for sleeping and rest.

Young Irish setters need attention and guidance if they are ▶ to become properly socialized. Just as the dam manages their early interaction with their littermates, you are responsible for teaching them how to behave with human beings.

Your puppy will have to adjust to being alone without its mother or its littermates. The puppy is not the only one who will have to make an adjustment. You will have one of your own and it is sometimes a difficult adjustment to make. You must remember that your new Irish setter puppy is soaking up information about you like a sponge. If you are inconsistent now, you will have to help your pup unlearn a number of things later. Unlearning is much harder than learning the right things in the first place.

You have made the conscious decision to share your home and life with an Irish setter. You have decided that crate training is the best way to regulate your young puppy when you cannot be with it. You have reached your first key point in the ownership of this dog. If you or some member of your family constantly responds to whining, crying, or any of the pitiful little noises a lonely puppy can make, you will train the puppy that these noises will get the desired response. Your Irish setter may just be a young puppy, but it can figure this lesson out quickly.

Although the whimpering of a puppy the first few nights is sad to hear, unless you want that whimpering to become a reinforced behavior, you must be firm. The puppy must learn that there is a time of interaction with its family and a time when quiet and sleep is required. A sad, lonely, crying puppy can become a sad, lonely, crying adult if you give in to sentiment and take the pup out of its special sleeping place and cuddle it every time it cries. Steel yourself and your family with the knowledge that your puppy will not continue to cry much beyond the first few days and that consistent firmness now will mean a much happier and better adjusted companion later.

Irish setters take to water with the same verve they display in the field. Most are strong swimmers—a characteristic that stood them in good stead during their development as a hunting dog.

You can help make this temporary ordeal somewhat easier for your puppy. Use an old-fashioned hot water bottle (with no leaks to mess up the den) to give the puppy a sense of warmth like it would have had with its mother. If you were able to bring an old piece of bedding or something from the breeder's for the "home" scent, so much the better. Some people place an old wind-up clock (alarm deactivated) in the den so that its ticking can simulate the beating of the mother's heart. Others have had success turning a radio on low volume, especially on an all night talk station. It seems just the sound is comforting to a young puppy and helps it fall asleep.

Your puppy also should be kept on the diet and feeding schedule that it had at the breeder's. You can make a change later. Unless the breeder has been experiencing food-related problems (which is unlikely for a knowledgeable breeder), stay with this diet. Even with the same food, a puppy may experience some mild diarrhea. Because your veterinarian has checked this puppy out thoroughly before you brought it home, you know this diarrhea is probably a transitional problem. If, however, the diarrhea continues for more than a few days, revisit the veterinarian with the puppy just to be safe.

Be sure that your Irish setter puppy gets plenty of exercise, but don't let it overexert itself. Your Irish setter is still a puppy and can play only in short spurts. These are days of initial leaning and adjustment. It is good to take things slow with the puppy and don't expect anything approaching mature behavior. Such behavior will come, but only in its own good time.

Traveling with Your Irish Setter

Although there are vacations and trips that may not lend themselves to the presence of a large, exuberant red dog, there are many other outings where your Irish setter can be a welcomed companion. A little foresight and planning can turn these junkets into pleasurable rather than miserable experiences. Your first concern always must be the safety, comfort, and needs of the dog.

Traveling by Car

Many of the activities (shows, field, and obedience trials) in which Irish setters participate involve a good deal of travel, especially by automobile. Good canine car safety is therefore a crucial part of any such activity. There are some good rules for you to follow when driving (even for a short distance) with your Irish setter.

Always, while in an automobile, have your pet restrained in some way. Many show people make a point to always use carriers when transporting their dogs. Although you cannot interact as well with your dog when it is in a carrier, you will not be distracted as easily. In the case of an accident, an unrestrained Irish setter can become a large, red, living missile that can collide with people or car interiors with great velocity. Other traveling dog owners use doggy seat belts that can be attached to regular auto belts to restrain their dogs.

Never let your Irish setter ride with its head out the car window. This may be enjoyable to the dog and look enjoyable to the owner, but it is a dangerous practice. The squashed bugs that decorate the grill and windshield can strike a dog's eye and possibly do considerable damage. In addition to bugs, the debris (rocks, pebbles) kicked up by other vehicles can blind a dog if the "road shrapnel" happens to hit an eye. Diesel and other fumes can't be good for a dog's respiration.

Never leave your dog in a parked car (even with the windows rolled down) on a day when the outside temperature is as high as 60°F (16°C). To do so is to sign your pet's death warrant in all too many cases. Death can claim an Irish setter in a surprisingly short time in that unventilated, overheated solar oven called the family car (see Heatstroke, page 51).

Allowing dogs to ride unrestrained in the back of an open pickup truck in another very dangerous

practice. Not only can the dog be thrown about (or out) but if you should stop at a stop sign when something chaseable is nearby, your dog may disembark and you may not even notice. Use a carrier or a dog box made to fit a pickup. As a last resort, there are restraints that are attached in the truck bed to which the dog is tethered. Although such devices may work, too long a lead or tether could result in a dog being bounced from the truck and being hung by the very device that was supposed to keep it safe.

Check with your veterinarian about motion sickness pills for your dog. It is usually not wise to feed it four to six hours prior to leaving and don't provide water less than two hours prior to departure.

On an extended trip of several hours, stop every hour or so to give the dog a breather, a brief drink of water, and a stretch. *Always* use a lead and collar when taking a dog out of the car in a strange locale.

If you utilize the rest areas on the interstate highway system, follow the rules. Don't allow your dog to relieve itself in areas other than those designated for this purpose. Always maintain control of even a well-trained dog during these breaks.

Check with auto clubs and travel guides about which motels and hotels will allow pets. When you confirm your itinerary and reservations, make sure that these rulings are still in force.

Before going into another state or province, you might be wise to have your dog's license and medical records with you along with a snapshot of the dog in case it gets lost. Also for an extended stay in another locale, you should call the health authorities in that area to learn of any special conditions that might affect your Irish setter's presence there.

Traveling by Plane

Air travel for pets certainly has changed in the past couple of decades. In the past, you put your pet's life in some danger whenever you traveled, because the airlines were not very understanding or sympathetic of live baggage. Today, your Irish

Caring for Your Irish Setter

setter, in an approved carrier, is welcome on most larger domestic and overseas airlines. There are still some good rules to follow before your Irish setter ever leaves the ground.

When you make your flight reservations, make certain that you fully discuss with the airline all their regulations and policies pertaining to taking your large dog along. (Always get the names of any people with whom you speak.)

Have your Irish setter checked out by your veterinarian. He or she also can provide you with the health certificate that has now become an almost universal requirement of airlines. This certificate must be dated not more than 10 days prior to your departure date. Some dogs may not be good travelers and your veterinarian can recommend whether your pet should stay home or if it will need tranquilizers or anti-airsick pills.

Make *early* your watchword. Make the reservations for you and your pet as far ahead of time as possible. Arrive extra early at the airline for both your outgoing and return flights.

You may want to drive to the nearest airline hub in order to get a direct flight to your ultimate destination. By eliminating changing fights, you also lessen the chances of your pet ending up at a different location than yours. By all means fly on the same flight as your pet, even if you have to take a different plane or airline than you planned.

Pre-flight check your airline-approved carrier. Make certain that all nuts and bolts are in place and are tight. Make sure that the door and latch are in good operating order and have a small padlock, and that the "airline conversion kit," which allows the pet to be watered from outside the carrier, is in place. Make sure that "Live Animal" stickers are prominently displayed, as well as your name, home address, and a telephone number where you can be reached in your destination city.

Be sure to put a freshly laundered blanket or pad into the carrier to make traveling more comfortable for your pet. A favorite toy or some long-lasting chew also would be a thoughtful addition.

Water and exercise your Irish setter about two hours before boarding the plane. Other than the conversion kit waterer, don't put food or water in the carrier as it could become a mess and uncomfortable for your dog.

Make certain that you have, packed away in your own bags, enough food and any medications your dog may need during the vacation. You may not be able to find the same food in your destination city.

In dealing with airline personnel, you should be polite, but firm. You must impress upon them in the nicest, but firmest way possible that your Irish setter is important to you and that you will go to great lengths to ensure its safety and comfort.

Boarding Your Irish Setter

Boarding your dog can be a good alternative to the rigors and possible difficulties of traveling with a pet. By dealing with this eventuality prior to having to actually board the dog, you will make the whole experience much less of an ordeal. There are several possibilities.

In most cities, there are pet sitters who are available to take care of your pet *in your own home,* when you are out of town. Usually, these are caring, skillful pet people (with references, of course) who can take good care of your pet. It is always advisable to have these sitters visit in your home with your Irish setter before you actually go on your trip.

For some traveling Irish setter owners, their regular veterinarian can board their pet. There is much to recommend this approach, for your dog will have the professional care by people who know the dog and whom it knows.

You may have family, friends, or neighbors who may be able to stay in your home and care for your pet on its own turf.

There are many quality boarding kennels across the country. These kennels are accredited with the American Boarding Kennel Association (ABKA) (see Useful Addresses and Literature, page 73).

Feeding Your Irish Setter

The Importance of a Balanced Diet

The importance of a balanced diet (and your complete understanding of what goes into such diet) cannot be overestimated. As one Irish setter admirer bluntly put it, "To get more out of your dog, you have to put more into your dog." Although this enthusiast was referring to a number of areas (care, training, and so on), feeding certainly fits this axiom perfectly. Computer people have a similarly fitting phrase, "Garbage In: Garbage Out."

As a rule, there are two major factors regulating a successful feeding program for your dog. To avoid a poor diet and establish a nutritionally-sound feeding plan, follow these two main principles:
• Feed your Irish setter a premium quality, nutritionally balanced dog food (understanding why it is such).
• Don't overfeed your Irish setter, allowing for this exuberant, active dog to have plenty of good exercise.

The important term here is balanced diet. A balanced diet is one that is nutritionally complete.

A quality dog food, fed in a knowledgeable and consistent manner, will amply meet your dog's nutritional needs. (Avoid table scraps!)

Your dog will do much better on a diet that provides all of the necessary elements to build strong bones, hair, teeth, muscle, and all of the other things that go into making up a healthy Irish setter. In order for you to recognize and understand what a balanced diet is and how it works (and how it can unintentionally be short-circuited), some discussion of basic canine nutrition is needed.

Basic Nutrition

There are seven components or aspects that go to make up a nutritionally complete or balanced diet for your Irish setter: proteins; carbohydrates; fats; vitamins; minerals; fresh, clean drinking water; and your knowledge of and consistency in feeding your dog. If any one of these parts is neglected or ignored, your dog's diet cannot be described as either balanced or complete.

Protein

Protein provides your Irish setter with the important amino acids that are so necessary for:
• normal growth throughout the formative stages of your dog's life;
• the sustained maintenance of healthy bone and healthy muscle;
• the body's own repair functions on that same bone and muscle;
• the production of infection-fighting antibodies; and
• the production of hormones and enzymes that aid in the dog's normal bodily chemical processes.

Good sources of protein commonly found in premium dog foods are: meat and poultry products, milk products, fish meal, soybeans, and corn. Protein is important to the makeup of any good dog food and is widely touted in ads and in brochures about the respective feeds. Your discussions with successful Irish setter breeders and your veterinarian, and through your own observation, will help you determine the levels of and best sources of protein in your Irish setter's food. Protein needs will change depending on the different growth phases of your dog. You will need to understand and recognize the needs of your puppy, adult dog, and older dog as it goes through each stage.

Carbohydrates

Carbohydrates provide energy to power your Irish setter's internal engine. Thoroughly cooked grain products, vegetable matter, and processed starches provide the greatest portion of the carbohydrates formulated into premium dog foods today. Carbohydrates generally vie with fats as energy providers in quality dog foods and are measured by caloric count or simply in calories.

Fats

Fats, like carbohydrates, provide energy to your Irish setter. They differ from carbohydrates in that fats provide a much more concentrated source of energy. In fact, the same amount of fat will provide *twice* as much usable energy as a like amount of carbohydrates. Fats also serve as the delivery system for vitamins A, D, E, and K throughout your setter's body. As such, A, D, E, and K are known as fat soluble vitamins and are useful in promoting healthy skin and coat. Fats also go into helping sustain and maintain a healthy nervous system. Lastly, but certainly not unimportantly, fats are utilized to make dog foods more tasty and palatable to dogs. You often see fats and protein viewed by breeders in a tandem role when dogs are used in any energy-expending or muscle-utilizing activity, like hunting, obedience trials, or in intense showroom competition.

Vitamins

Vitamins needed by your Irish setter for general body functions usually are needed only in small quantities, which are supplied easily in a balanced diet of a premium dog food. Because you are using premium food that is nutritionally complete, additional vitamins in the form of diet supplementation are *not* required generally (and may even be

contraindicated). The very best source of the vitamins your dog will need will be in a well-balanced diet.

Minerals

Minerals are essential for normal canine body functioning:
• Calcium and phosphorus are needed for the development and maintenance of strong bones, muscles, and teeth.
• Sodium and potassium aid in the maintenance of normal bodily fluids and with maintaining a healthy nervous system.
• Iron is utilized to promote healthy blood in your Irish setter in the process of transporting oxygen throughout the dog's body.

Minerals, like vitamins, are not needed in huge amounts in the normal canine diet. Your use of a premium-grade dog food generally will provide the specific amounts of minerals that your dog's body can and will need. As with vitamins, minerals easily can be overused. Before trying to add vitamins or minerals to your Irish setter's regular diet of a premium food, consult with your veterinarian.

Water

One of the most important parts of your Irish setter's balanced diet, and yet an often underemphasized part, is the need for pure, fresh water. Your setter will need plenty of good water at all times.

Water that is not fresh, but bacteria- or algae-laden, will not be utilized in the needed amounts by your dog. Treat water as you would any other key element in your dog's well-being. Keep water bowls clean, disinfected, and full of fresh water as often as possible.

Consistency/Knowledge

Although all the components of basic nutrition are important, none is more important than your own efforts to understand what you should feed your Irish setter and why. Your dog will be totally dependent on you for its food. If you do well in this, your dog will thrive. If you don't, your dog will not do as well as it could have.

Your understanding of what goes into a premium food and why such a food constitutes a balanced, nutritionally complete diet for your Irish setter will make you a better provider for your red dog. You will see that not every product that receives widespread advertising will give you what you will want and what your Irish setter will need in a dog food.

Commercial Dog Food

There are a number of excellent high-quality dog foods on the market today. There are an even greater number of products masquerading as high-quality dog foods trying to capture your attention and your dog food dollars. Your goal is to discover the difference.

One of the best things that you, as a dog food purchaser (if not an actual dog food consumer) can learn is how to read the labels and the lists of ingredients on the containers of food you are considering. These ingredients are required, by law, to be listed in order of percentage. The ingredient that makes up the greatest portion of the food is listed first. The second highest percentage ingredient is listed next and so forth down through the food items into the vitamins, minerals, and trace ingredients.

Learning to read the labels and ingredient lists will give you a good overview of the way in which this or that dog food is manufactured. After the first three or four ingredients, most of the remaining items are in really such small amounts as to be out of the mainstream when talking about the formulation of the food. For example, if "chicken, corn, rice…" are the first three food ingredients and other items like "beef, lamb…" are eighth and ninth on the ingredients ladder, it would not be really truthful to call this food a beef-based or lamb-based diet. It is, in effect, a diet in which chicken, corn, and rice

are the predominant food items. Chicken, for example, may make up 35 percent of the food, corn may be 29 percent, and rice in this mixture may be 21 percent. These three total 85 percent with all the remaining ingredients combining to make up the remaining 15 percent.

Also on the label should be the manufacturer's recommended feeding amounts based on weight. These are generally ballpark figures and do not represent the fine tuning that you may be able to ultimately accomplish for your Irish setter. Talk with veteran setter breeders, your veterinarian, and perhaps a canine nutritionist (usually available through the premium dog food companies' "1-800" numbers). Remember that your Irish setter will need different amounts of different formulations of quality dog food at different times in its life.

Premium food may be a bit more expensive initially, but as most professional dog breeders will tell you, it will be much cheaper in the long run. Premium foods have clear, easy to understand ingredient lists. They have high consistency and quality control standards. (The food you bought last week will be the same as you will buy next week.) They generally have excellent canine research data to back up their nutritional approaches.

Premium quality dog food companies spend millions of dollars each year to make certain that their products are the best they can make them. These products generally are marketed through specialty sources like veterinarians, pet and pet supply stores, some feed stores, and some groomers. Their investment in quality nutrition can pay off in a balanced diet and good health for your Irish setter. Your dog may live if fed the cheapest foods around, but you hardly could expect it to thrive and be the type of pet you are seeking on a substandard diet.

Commercial dog foods have become a big business. You should realize that *you* are the target for many of the ads and promotions that appear each year. Don't purchase a food for your Irish setter because of a cute advertisement, or because your

Feeding Your Irish Setter

favorite color is on their bag, or because it is on sale. Study the available products and find a food that fits your Irish setter's needs.

Commercial dog foods generally are produced in three main forms: dry, semimoist, and canned. Each type has its advantages and disadvantages.

Dry

The most popular form of dog food is dry. There are a number of advantages to a high-quality dry food. The most important is the existence of nutritionally complete dry dog food diets. These are the balanced diets that have so much to offer your Irish setter.

In addition to being nutritionally complete, dry dog foods keep well without refrigeration. They are usually good in palatability (their only real drawback is that some dogs have to be taught or retaught to eat some of them). Your dog's teeth will be in better shape with a dry food that actually helps clear tartar and clean the teeth and gums.

High-quality dry foods are usually the most economical of all commercial types (a point not lost on the breeders of large dogs like the Irish setter). With premium quality dog food, you will feed only about half as much as you would with a food of lesser quality. They are easily fed and have achieved good palatability and canine acceptance. Dry dog food will, however, have a moisture rating of only about 10 percent. This makes the provision of lots of clean, fresh water for your Irish setter that much more important.

Semimoist

Semimoist dog food often comes in burger shapes or in other meat looking configurations and colors. It is very palatable and very convenient. The cost is generally higher than dry foods and stool firmness is not as good as with a premium dry food. Semimoist foods can be used for trips and for times when your dog's appetite may be a little sluggish. Semimoist foods have a moisture rating of about 30 percent.

Canned

Canned dog food is the most expensive way to feed a dog. It is also quite palatable, but due to its high moisture rating of between 75 to 85 percent, it can spoil quickly, even at room temperature. Canned food, if fed exclusively, can lead to weight problems like obesity. Stool firmness is not very good with canned dog foods and these stools generally have a much more noxious odor than other forms produce. Canned food can be convenient and its shelf life is exceptional. For a large breed, like Irish setters, canned food isn't very cost effective, though some dog owners occasionally mix it with their dry dog food.

Homemade Diets

Some dog owners do considerable concocting in an effort to give their pet the best possible diet. This may seem to be a harmless individual preference, but such is *not* the case. Unless you are a trained animal nutritionist or a dog breeder with years and years of experience, homemade diets are not a good idea for your dog! As in the discussion with vitamins and minerals, it is quite easy to unbalance your dog's diet. With the large number of excellent commercial dog foods on the market today, making your own seems to be both an extra effort and a risky nutritional proposition for your Irish setter!

Treats

As a rule, table scraps have *no* place in a nutritionally complete pet food diet. No matter how appealing it may be to share food from your own table with your Irish setter, avoid it. Your Irish setter needs a diet that is nutritionally complete for a dog—*not* for a human! In addition to throwing your dog's diet out of balance, feeding table scraps can encourage the bad habit of begging for tidbits while you are having dinner.

Among treats that *can* be given safely to your dog without a danger of causing dietary imbalance are quality dog biscuits. These not only are nutri-

35

tionally good for your dog, but they have the added benefit of helping to clean your dog's teeth and gums.

Other chews, like the various rawhide and nylon items, are good for teething Irish setter pups as well as adult dogs who like the taste. Because of their high activity levels, Irish setters really can benefit from some strong chew toys. The energy burned off gnawing on these will save your Irish setter from boredom (which often can lead to trouble) and you from having something chewed on that is not meant for that purpose!

If you feed a high-quality, dry dog food, there is a way that you can give your dog a treat without upsetting its diet. Put some of the dry food in a microwave safe bowl. Add just a couple tablespoons of water. Microwave this dish of food for about 30 to 45 seconds on high. Allow the food to cool thoroughly. The nutritional values remain much the same, but fats in the dry food have been pulled to the outside. This will give the regular dog food a different taste, not unlike the difference in a charbroiled hamburger and one cooked in a pan on top of the stove. (Hint: Don't use too much water or you will run the risk of losing stool firmness.)

Feeding Puppies (One Year Old and Younger)

The Irish setter is a relatively slow maturing breed. This means that you may have to continue to feed the higher protein and fat diet that puppies need for a little longer than you would with some other types of dogs. How you feed your Irish setter puppy will have a profound impact on the dog that puppy grows up to be. Puppies need a nutritionally complete diet formulated especially for the stresses and needs of growing young dogs. In fact, puppies generally need *twice* as much in nutrition as adult dogs do.

For your Irish setter puppy, utilize the very best puppy food available. Feed this food in a consistent

manner and your puppy will have the strong foundation it will need to be a healthy, active adult Irish setter. Skimp on puppy food and you are throwing open the door to a myriad of physical, mental, and developmental problems. Your puppy will need to be fed three or four times each day on a regular schedule. At six months, you should be able to cut back on feeding times to two or three times per day. Of course, the amount of food or number of times per day you feed will not mean much if you are not feeding a puppy food of the highest quality. To repeat a previously mentioned statement, "To get more out of your dog, you have to put more into your dog."

There does exist some difference of opinion among dog breeders of large, rapidly-developing breeds about the amount of protein needed in a puppy's diet. Some say that excessive amounts of protein can cause muscles and tissue to develop more quickly than bones and skeletal structure. The result, these people say, is a bowing effect on the legs of puppies in such breeds as Great Danes. Discuss this possibility with veteran Irish setter breeders and with your veterinarian. The slower maturity rate in Irish setters does seem to make this less of a problem, or no problem at all in the breed.

Feeding Adult Dogs (Over One Year Old)

As your puppy reaches physical maturity at around eighteen months to two years of age, its nutritional needs will evolve from those of a growing puppy to those of an adult male or female Irish setter. Two feedings per day of a high-quality dog food designed for adult dogs will now generally suffice.

Field trials or hunting, obedience work, showing, and breeding will all require more in the form of good nutrition than the amounts needed by most backyard pets. On a good diet, your Irish setter should have fairly consistent nutritional needs from

Feeding Your Irish Setter

about eighteen months or two years up to about age eight. These needs will require a food that will power your dog through his middle years. Of course, if your Irish setter is spayed or neutered, regardless of age, you should feed it like an older dog.

Feeding Older Dogs (Eight Years Old and Older)

When your Irish setter gets to be eight years old or so (some dogs age faster or slower than the norm), its metabolic rate will begin to slow down. A dog at this point in its life usually will need less energy, thus less fat and less protein. (Of course, those individuals still involved in physically demanding activities like breeding, hunting, and showing will still need a diet with ample energy providing ingredients.)

Generally speaking, older dogs (and spayed or neutered dogs), if kept on a higher energy diet in the same amounts, will tend to put on too much weight. Overweight dogs are not healthy dogs in the strictest sense of the word.

Sadly, dog owners are sometimes very hard to convince when they are told that their older dog will need less food in its later years. Dog nutritionists and veterinarians commonly hear, "But Rusty *always* gets two full cups of dog food." Rusty may have needed this amount of food earlier in life, but overfeeding can be a very negative, albeit unintentional, thing to do to one's dog.

In response to this age group, most of the premium quality dog food manufacturers now have foods formulated for older or spayed and neutered dogs. Consult with your veterinarian or use the "1-800" number of the company that makes the premium food your Irish setter has been eating up to this point. These resources should be able to not only suggest some light diets for dogs whose metabolism is now less active than before, but also explain why this or that food would be better.

On any dietetic difficulties, like allergies, your veterinarian always will be your best ally. You can, of course, help prevent many diet-related problems by starting your Irish setter on quality food and continuing this practice for the dog's entire life. Premium quality food will not be a luxury item but an indispensable part of Irish setter ownership.

Changing from One Dog Food to Another

Changes in dog food should not be undertaken casually or often. Your dog will do much better on a long-term, consistent, high-quality feeding program than on a constantly changing diet. Don't use your dog as a "food testing facility"!

Dog food changes should occur gradually, the longer the change, the better. One way to change foods (and this relates to changing brands or changing from puppy to adult, for example) is to begin a percentage decrease of the old food. For a couple of days, you feed 75 percent of the old food with 25 percent of the new. Then for two more days, feed 50 percent of each. Finally, for several days (or until the old food is gone), feed 75 percent of the new in a mixture containing 25 percent of the old.

Grooming and Your Irish Setter

Grooming and the Irish Setter— An Overview

The Irish setter is not a difficult breed to groom. Although some differences do exist, grooming techniques for a show Irish setter and your pet are much the same. Due to the relative simplicity of such grooming and also because owning an Irish setter is, at least in part, a visual experience, you should give your dog good grooming attention.

Show grooming will of course require more of you than your pet's at-home appearance will demand. There is, however, no reason not to have your Irish setter looking reasonably good all the time. Your Irish setter will deserve this attention and you will come to enjoy the time you and your dog spend in this activity. Begin grooming early in a pup's life to make the process less threatening and more easily accomplished later on.

Grooming an exhibition Irish setter will call for several things on your part:
• knowledge of the Irish setter standard as it pertains to coat quality, permissible trimming, and so on;
• the right grooming equipment to use and a good understanding of how to use it;
• some on-the-job training in Irish setter grooming from an experienced breeder or a professional groomer (it is much better and easier to spend a lot of time in training than even a brief time in regret);
• an understanding of shampoos, rinses, and the best techniques in their use;
• an appraisal of your dog's coat from a qualified Irish setter breeder or groomer with emphasis on any specific concerns or problems that may exist.

The Irish Setter Standard as It Pertains to the Coat

The approved standard says: "Coat: Short and fine on head, forelegs, and tips of ears; on all other parts, of moderate length and flat. Feathering long

Regular brushing will keep your Irish setter looking good and will be a good experience for both of you.

and silky on ears; on back of forelegs and thighs long and fine, with a pleasing fringe of hair on belly and brisket extending onto the chest. Feet well feathered between the toes. Fringe on tail moderately long and tapering. All coat and feathering as straight and free as possible from curl or wave."

Grooming Equipment

The first equipment to consider is a good set of clippers (Oster models A-2 or A-5 are most often mentioned by Irish setter breeders). Scissors are the next item to obtain. There are two kinds of scissors needed: thinners (for removing extra coat on the back legs and general blending); straight scissors (used on the feet, toes, and muzzle whiskers).

Another Irish setter grooming aid will be stripping combs or strippers. These come in a variety of styles (and prices) and are used to strip the coat of old hair. Your breeder or a professional groomer

Grooming and Your Irish Setter

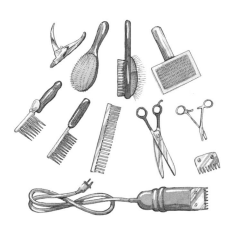

Your Irish setter's coat can be kept in good shape by proper and regular use of wire and bristle brushes, tangle removers, stripping combs, scissors, clippers, and a wire slicker.

can best help you with the kind that best fits the coat of your Irish setter.

Brushes are of three types: natural bristle for overall coat care; wider pin brush (a brush utilizing blunt metal pins mounted in a rubber face) for separating the long feathering area; and slicker brush (like the wire or pin brush, but much finer pins are used) for light brushing of coat and heavier feathered area.

Combs, usually with metal or wooden handles, are also part of your Irish setter grooming kit. Purchase a comb with wide teeth gaps and with graduated lengths of teeth. This will be used on the coat to keep it in good line. As with all the grooming tools, it is best to get a good breeder or professional groomer to show you how to most effectively use the combs.

Nail trimmers are another necessary tool in grooming. There are two types available: the plier type, which, as it sounds, cuts the nail from both sides like a pair of pincers; and the guillotine, which

has an opening into which the nail is placed and a blade that moves across cutting the nail. Care must be taken with both types of nail trimmers not to "hit the quick" of the nail (cutting too deeply can cause bleeding). You will also want a metal file and one of the various blood-stopping powders (for example, Kwik-stop) in the event that you do cause bleeding while trimming the dog's nails.

A final area of grooming involves your dog's teeth. There are a number of good canine dental kits on the market. Ask your veterinarian or pet store to recommend one. Good preventive dental care will help keep your Irish setter more pleasant to be around, but also will help keep the dog healthy.

Grooming the Show Irish Setter

Show dogs are regularly bathed, as often as weekly. Thorough brushing usually is done about

To remove grease or tar from your Irish setter's coat, rub with margarine, mayonnaise, or salad oil. If a residue of tar remains, trim it off with scissors. Do not use bleach or harsh cleansers.

twice a week. When you brush your Irish setter for exhibition purposes, use a spray-mist bottle to moisten the coat. It is never advisable to brush (for show) a completely dry Irish setter. Using your natural bristle brush, brush in the direction that coat hair naturally follows. Never tear at the coat, for this destroys new hair development.

Find a professional groomer or Irish setter breeder/exhibitor to teach you the fine points of trimming and general show grooming. Your efforts at keeping your show dog well manicured and well groomed will be in keeping the with dog's natural beauty.

Grooming and Your Pet Irish Setter

Although the bathing requirements for a nonshow dog may be less than for a show dog, a good shampoo will be needed from time to time. Brushing should be a weekly activity and trimming can be done on an as-needed basis.

Even a pet-quality Irish setter is an elegant and beautiful dog. Good regular grooming will only enhance your dog's appearance. Without this care, your Irish setter's coat may become matted or even sloppy looking. Regular brushing, and bathing will be a good experience for both you and the dog.

Raising Quality Irish Setters

Reasons, Realities, and Responsibilities

The decision to allow a litter of puppies to be born should be considered carefully in all instances and most certainly in the case of the Irish setter. Casual breeding of dogs is not a recommended practice for even experienced dog people and certainly not for beginners. Irish setters are beautiful, spirited, and often quite prolific. On the off chance that you are a breeder-waiting-to-be, there are any number of things you should ponder.

Remember the depth of self-examination recommended before you bought your Irish setter puppy? Before you decide to produce more Irish setters, you would be well advised to triple your introspection. Always ask yourself "Why do I want to raise Irish setters?"

If you just want to let your setter bitch go through the joys of maternal bliss, do her and yourself a big favor and forget it. An admittedly beautiful scene of your pet nursing her pups will get old pretty quick when you consider that Irish setters often have very large litters. If your bitch has more pups than she can handle, guess who has to step into the void and hand-feed the remaining hungry puppies, every four hours? You do!

Irish setters are generally good mothers and can do very well in the whelping box, but does your bitch really need this experience to make her a better pet? Even if she is physically fit, produces and raises only an average litter, a litter of puppies will be a drain on the health of any bitch.

If you want your children to have the experience of helping to raise some puppies (as if your initial Irish setter wasn't sufficient experience), perhaps you can take them to a breeder who may welcome your children's help in socializing a litter of growing setters.

Hopefully you won't consider raising Irish setters for an unlimited wealth market. Such a fantasy isn't just wishful thinking—it's a pure pipe dream.

Most dog breeders will quickly tell you that there is a lot more outgo than income in raising even top-of-the-line, high-quality show dogs.

Before you allow 10 or 12 (or more) Irish setter puppies to come into the world, a good question to ask yourself is "What am I going to do with all these puppies?" You could, of course, keep them all and add your dog food store to your list of major creditors. You could attempt to sell them, but we've discussed some aspects of that option. You could parcel them out to family and friends (the family may even speak to you again someday). One thing every responsible dog breeder should always do is to take responsibility for any and all puppies they raise for those puppies' *entire* lives. They didn't ask to be brought into the world; you made that decision. You must honor it and stand by it.

Irish setters are large dogs with special needs for good care, good food, plenty of exercise. If you can't guarantee *each* puppy a home where it will get all of these things and an optimum of love, then you shouldn't breed Irish setters. A number of Irish setter breeders have "horror stories" about having sold or even given a puppy to an apparently wonderful family only to have that puppy live an existence of unmitigated hell. In many of these cases these puppies have to be reclaimed, placed in another environment, or even mercifully put to sleep.

If your reasons for breeding Irish setters have their basis in some ego need to be thought of as a dog breeder, there is a better and easier way. Buy the very best Irish setter puppy you can from the very best show strain available. You can nurture the puppy into a fine young dog. If you are willing to learn (and are lucky), you may be able to campaign it right to an AKC championship or to an advanced obedience title or perhaps both. That's where the status is with dogs and if your ego can stand the trip, it's a ride to remember.

One final point to consider before you breed your dog is the large number of unwanted puppies that are born each year. Many of these come to tragic ends. Unless you are *absolutely* certain about the future of any Irish setters you cause to be born, don't add to the problem and to the suffering.

For those few to whom the challenge of striving for canine betterment is a must, there are proven ways to go about it. Become a serious student of Irish setters, their lineage, possible problems, and general dog care. Continue your learning by talking with and getting to know as many Irish setter breeders as possible. Listen to these breeders. Read and reread the Irish setter standard until you know it by heart. Study canine genetics and learn about dog breeding in depth. Examine your financial situation (breeding quality Irish setters won't be an inexpensive proposition, even for one litter). Have your dog evaluated by an impartial third party (exhibiting your dog to a championship could be acceptable proof of breeding potential).

Most importantly, have your veterinarian assess the overall health and physical condition of your dog as potential breeding stock. You should have your dog's hips, eyes, and possibly other areas checked for any conditions that may be genetic in origin and thus could be passed along. Ask for and expect a candid appraisal from your veterinarian. Follow his or her findings.

Lastly, before you make your final decision about breeding your dog and producing more puppies, go down to your local animal shelter. Take a good close look at all those adorable dogs and puppies and recognize that a vast majority of them *never* will be adopted. You should then realize that the decision to breed dogs is not one to be made lightly.

The Estrous Cycle

A female Irish setter usually will come into season (or in heat) approximately every six months. This is known as the estrous cycle and should occur the first time when she is between six and eight months of age. There may be some slight variation in the estrous cycle from bitch to bitch or from breed to breed.

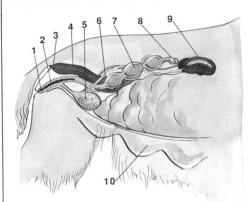

The reproductive system of a female Irish setter:
1. vulva
2. anus
3. vagina
4. rectum
5. bladder
6. ureter
7. developing embryo
8. ovaries
9. kidneys
10. mammary glands

Normally the estrous cycle will be marked by several phases:
• Proestrus, or the preparation part of the cycle, is marked by the onset of activity of the uterus and in the ovaries. The ovaries are producing ova or eggs. As these eggs mature, the uterus thickens and a blood-tinged vaginal discharge can be observed. Proestrus lasts an average of nine days (but can be as short as four days or as long as almost two weeks). Your female will attract male dogs during proestrus, but will not be ready to mate with them. The vulva or external female genital organ will swell during proestrus.
• Estrus is the second phase of the estrous cycle. It follows closely behind proestrus. In estrus, the vaginal discharge is not as bloody and will take on a clear color and thin, mucus-like consistency. Male dogs will continue to be attracted to the bitch during estrus and actual mating can take place during this phase. Ovulation takes place during estrus and usually occurs between the ninth and fourteenth day (dating from the onset of proestrus). Estrus will last

about the same length of time as did proestrus, with pregnancy possible throughout the average nine-day time period.

• If your Irish setter female has received a male (mated) during estrus, for the next six to eight weeks the metestrus phase occurs. In metestrus, the mammary glands evolve toward lactation or milk production.

• Metestrus ends with the beginning of anestrus (the last stage of the estrous cycle), where the bitch's ovaries and uterus begin to return to their initial pre-estrous cycle form.

• If not mated during estrus, the female's system gradually will go "out of heat" and a shrinking of the vulva, cessation of discharge, and ovarian inactivity will be observed. She will stay in this form until the cycle starts again in five and a half to six months.

As a general health rule, your bitch should not be allowed to become pregnant until her third regular heat at between eighteen to twenty months of age.

During the estrous cycle, you will have the added responsibility of keeping your female Irish setter away from male dogs. This will involve keeping her from contact and from sight. Don't count on a fenced-in backyard to keep two (or more) romantic dogs from getting together. Worse than having an unwanted litter of purebred Irish setters is the prospect of having an unwanted litter of half-bred Irish setters.

The Stud Dog

If you have given careful thought to the negatives surrounding dog breeding and have determined that you really want to pursue it, your next objective is to find a compatible male for your female. You should have begun this process well in advance of the projected mating time. You (and your experienced Irish setter breeder-advisors) will have studied your female's pedigree and that of several potential males. Your goal here is to find a male that will blend his genetic qualities with those of your female. This male *must* be a superior speci-

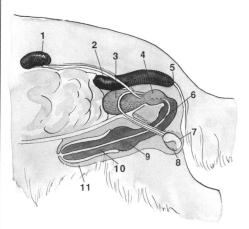

The reproductive system of a male Irish setter:

1. kidneys	7. scrotum
2. rectum	8. testes
3. bladder	9. bulb
4. prostate	10. penis
5. anus	11. sheath
6. urethra	

men. Under most circumstances, the stud should be a show champion with all of the personality traits and strengths you want to see passed on in the offspring.

It goes without saying that neither the male nor the female should have any open (overt) or known hidden (covert) defects or flaws that can be transmitted genetically. The male should be at least one year old. If your female is a virgin, it would be better if the male had previous experience as a stud dog. Often a male will breed better at home and usually the female is taken to him.

You should have your female checked by a veterinarian for the presence of a venereally-transmitted, bacterial disease known as brucellosis, which can wreak havoc with breeding dogs. Brucellosis can cause aborted litters or even render the adult dogs sterile. Most serious breeders will require a written assurance from your veterinarian stating that your bitch is brucellosis-free.

You would be wise to have the stud fee (payment for the male's mating with your female) clearly stated in writing in advance. Usually a stud dog owner will want a set amount of money and/or their pick of a puppy out of the litter as payment. Irish setters normally have fairly large litters and a serious breeder who thinks enough of your bitch to want a puppy from her would be a good indicator as to her worth or potential as a breeder. Remember though, the pick of the litter could well be the only puppy with show potential in the entire litter!

Your arrangement with the owner of the stud dog should also include a guarantee that your bitch will conceive and bear puppies. If conception does not occur, you normally should be allowed to have your female re-mated to the stud dog at her next estrous cycle.

You may want to be on-site when the mating takes place. If you do not know the stud dog owner well, you may want to be sure that the exact male you have so painstakingly chosen for your female is the male who actually sires her puppies. Most breeders are honest, but you are new to the game and must take some reasonable precautions.

If you have failed to do your homework (in meeting Irish setter breeders, studying pedigrees, and so forth) and your female is not an excellent show-quality specimen, the stud dog owner may not allow her to be mated to his male. This is an appropriate and reasonable attitude. The male's owner will not want his stud to breed to a substandard female who probably will produce puppies closer to her lower level of quality rather than to that of his good male. Also a stud is judged by the excellence of the puppies he sires. If the male is bred to poor quality females, with the resultant poor quality litters as his only testimony, then the demand for his services will decrease. A stud's owner must try to breed his male to the very best females possible to enhance the chances that his dog will sire the next outstanding Irish setter. This underscores your need for the best possible Irish setter puppy when you start out.

Mating

You have devoted considerable thought and effort into this breeding. You will have your Irish setter in the best possible health prior to the onset of the estrous cycle. You will have gotten the necessary veterinarian approvals, had her wormed, and are sure her vaccinations are up-to-date. The genetic makeup of a good sire is of course important, but the best stud dog in the world cannot offset the negative impact of a bitch who is in poor condition.

As mentioned, the ovulating phase of the estrous cycle is estrus. Breeders generally will try to bring a female to the male on the ninth day of the cycle. Although some introductory time may be necessary, mating can take place very soon thereafter.

When copulating, the male and female may be tied or locked together by the action of the penis and vagina. This is a natural occurrence and will cease when the mating urges subside. Your female can become tied with the stud dog more than once during the two or so days of maximum receptibility. (Note: A female during this time also can mate with another male after the initial mating has taken place. To be absolutely certain of the puppies' parentage, it is important to keep her away from all other males until after estrous has ended!)

False Pregnancy

Sometimes a female will fail to conceive (or never be bred at all!) and yet take on many of the outward manifestations and behaviors common to actual pregnancy. This condition can be caused by ovarian cysts and related hormonal problems. Al-

Top: When teaching your Irish setter to heel, your pet ▶ should be on your left. Hold most of the leash in your right hand, but use the left hand to apply corrective tugs.
Bottom: Pull up on the leash as you push down on your dog's hindquarters to teach the "sit."

though recognized internal medical treatment can help, some bitches can develop pyometritis and related problems, which can require surgery for removal of her ovaries and uterus.

Pyometritis and similar disorders occur most often in females that have not had puppies. Don't ignore false pregnancy as it can have serious side effects. If your Irish setter female is pet quality and not a potential brood bitch, then have her spayed. Not only can she avoid many medical problems, but you also can avoid unwanted puppies.

Pregnancy

The usual gestation term for a pregnant female will be approximately 63 days after mating. At about the sixth week of this nine-week period, the female will begin to look pregnant with her abdomen swelling. About this time, her teats will become enlarged as they prepare for feeding hungry puppies.

Always give your Irish setter female tender, loving care, but especially so during her pregnancy and even more so if it is her first pregnancy. Her diet should be a nutritionally complete premium quality food. Many breeders even begin feeding a brood bitch puppy food to enhance her condition for producing and then raising a healthy litter. Exercise, too, is important for an Irish setter, and you want to be sure she is heavy with puppies and not just heavy with excess fat. It is not wise, however, to let her exercise be overly strenuous.

About two weeks before the puppies are due (if not sooner), you should separate her from other dogs. Avoid any rough play during this time and

◀ Once your Irish setter has mastered the basics, you may wish to try more challenging maneuvers. But whatever you are teaching, be patient, keep the sessions short, and offer lavish praise when the skill is mastered.

handle her with care. She should be allowed easy access to her den. Especially for a first litter, the female's emotional and physical well-being should be a prime concern.

The Whelping Box

As the time for the birth of the puppies nears, you should make certain that you have things ready for them. One thing to have, well in advance, is a whelping box. This is another instinctual carryover from the days when puppies were born in dens and lairs. It should be large enough for the female to be able to lie comfortably on her side. Not just for the whelping of the puppies, the whelping box must be large enough for her to raise the litter in for several weeks.

Whelping boxes can be homemade (be sure to follow some breeder's proven design) or purchased. It should be placed in an area that is out of drafts and where it can be warm, dry, and away from the beaten path. (As an active dog of some sensitivity, this is important for the Irish setter bitch's well-being.)

The box itself should be up off the floor (to avoid dampness or inordinate coolness). It should have sides low enough for easy access for the mother dog (and her often pendulous teats) and high enough to keep the puppies inside while they are very young. A shelf or rail several inches wide on the inside of the box will help keep puppies from inadvertently being trapped and crushed by their mother.

Line the whelping box with several layers of black and white printed newspapers (avoid ads or comics with colored inks that sometimes contain chemicals that might do newborn pups some harm). As the newspapers are dirtied, they can be removed easily.

Preparations for Whelping

Even as a first-time mother, an Irish setter bitch usually will have few problems, but if you are a

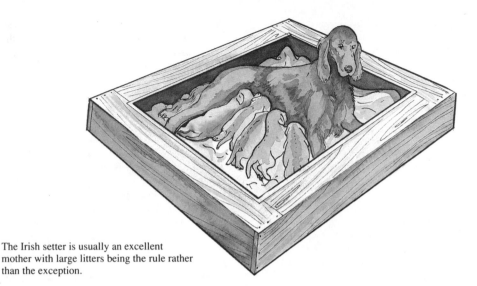

The Irish setter is usually an excellent mother with large litters being the rule rather than the exception.

first-time midwife, you may want to have your veterinarian either help with the delivery of the puppies or be on call if some problem occurs.

In the day preceding the puppies' arrival, the mother will become increasingly restless and somewhat anxious. She needs your tender loving care now, especially if this is her first litter. Plan to be with her in a quiet and reassuring way. Give her plenty of praise, and by your love, attitude and presence, let her know everything will be fine.

Before D-day (delivery) comes, talk with your veterinarian and perhaps a trusted Irish setter breeder about what to expect. If you are calm, you will convey this confidence to your Irish setter. If you are unsure of yourself, don't be ashamed to ask for help. Perhaps your trusted (and experienced) breeder friend will be on hand to help you and your dog.

Prepare for the birth day by getting all the needed supplies well in advance. You will need a heating pad and cloth-lined temporary box in which to place early arrivals while their brothers and sisters are being born, heavy surgical silk (dental floss will do just as well), and some sharp safety scissors to handle the umbilical cords. Some old towels or similar cloths will be needed to wipe off the emerging puppies.

Whelping

As the puppies are born, the mother usually will pull away the sac encasing each puppy and bite through the umbilical cord. If she doesn't do this, you should cut it, being careful to tie off each cord. As each puppy is born, the dam usually will clean it and prepare it to begin nursing.

Each birth should be followed by the afterbirth, which the bitch often will eat. (This is a normal and natural phenomenon that shouldn't cause her any harm.) Each birth normally will have the afterbirth. You should make certain that all afterbirths have been expelled from the mother's body. If you suspect that any have been retained, you should call your veterinarian.

Irish setters normally have quite large litters. The length of time between the first birth and the last could be in terms of a couple of hours or longer.

Raising Quality Irish Setters

Using your prepared box and heating pad, you can keep the firstborn puppies from becoming chilled while the later pups are being born.

Care of the Puppies

The Irish setter brood bitch is often a superb mother. She will give her litter excellent care during their first six weeks of life. Her milk will help the puppies get their first protection against the common dog diseases. After they reach six weeks of age, they will need the initial immunization series of shots from your veterinarian.

You can greatly help your Irish setter care for her pups by maintaining a consistent environment for them. During their first few weeks, the puppies will need to be kept warm at 80° to 90°F (27°–32°C). Very young puppies cannot adjust to cold temperatures or to violent shifts in temperature. The mother does what she can, but she needs your help.

After five weeks or so, the puppies will be better able to maintain their body temperature. If you use a heating source like a pad or a light, be sure that the heat is effective—neither too near or too far from the box. Also make certain that all wiring is safe and well out of reach of the puppies.

Under normal circumstances, the Irish setter mother dog will be the primary caregiver for her young. This is especially so the first few weeks of their lives. She washes them, feeds them, even cleans up after them. Your role has been one of preparation up to this point: keeping the mother healthy and well nourished; providing a warm, dry, safe environment without undue distractions; and standing by in case of difficulties. For the first month of their lives, the mother generally will do all the key tasks in raising the puppies.

If your Irish setter dam cannot care for her puppies or has too many puppies to care for adequately, you will have to step in to help her. Bottle feeding the puppies will be quite a chore. Using a milk replacer, suggested or provided by your veterinarian, you will need to feed each hungry little red puppy about every four hours of its first few weeks. Hungry Irish setter pups will loudly let you know they want to be fed by their whimpering and squealing. When their little red bellies are full, their loud protesting will cease. A large litter of Irish setters will be quite a job if bottle feeding is required. Hand-feeding puppies will greatly bond them with humans and socializing the puppies is much easier to accomplish.

Timely weaning of the puppies is of considerable importance to the mother. Because of the large litters Irish setter mothers often have, your help in gradually moving the puppies off an exclusive diet of mother's milk onto more solid fare is advisable. At about four to five weeks, you can begin introducing a high-quality, nutritionally complete, premium puppy food. You can start by adding lukewarm water to soften the puppy food. As the puppies mature, you can cut back on the amount of water until they are eating the food dry. (Note: This is *not* the time for a bargain basement mentality. Do the best you can do for your puppies by buying an excellent puppy food to get them off to the best possible start. You will not regret it.)

You can teach the puppies to eat the dry food by allowing bits of the moistened food to stick to your fingers. The puppies will smell the delicious scent on your fingers and will lick it off. Be sure you have a large, flat-bottomed dish that can accommodate the number of puppies. Don't feed them in the whelping box as the eating habits of 11 or 12 Irish setters will be less than tidy.

At six weeks, carefully load up your brood for a trip to the veterinarian. They will get a series of temporary shots and be checked for worms. Even though your puppies have only known the whelping box and nearby as their home, they can contract roundworms from their mother. Let the veterinarian prescribe the treatment for any worm infestations and follow the instructions.

At this age, Irish setter puppies are active red bundles of curiosity. Remembering the puppy-proofing you did when you brought your first setter puppy home, do the same safety check on any and all areas to which the litter of puppies will have access. If one puppy can get into trouble, imagine what 10 or 12 can do!

Socializing the Puppies

Socializing the puppies is an important and enjoyable job. Try to spend time with each puppy, even if you have to briefly separate it from the others. Don't just roughhouse either. Play can be active, but the goal here is to show the puppies that they need not fear human beings. Until now; you should have limited access to the puppies by neighbors and friends. You can now use the attentions of these friendly humans to teach the puppies about people other than those in your household.

At seven weeks, the litter can begin to go its separate ways to good homes that you hopefully have prequalified. In much the same way you went through the process of becoming an Irish setter owner, you must now reverse positions. Finding good homes for your good puppies could be the hardest part of the entire dog breeding experience.

Be an inquiring puppy breeder. At some point in every dog breeder's life there comes a time, if only for a brief moment, when disposing of the puppies becomes a desperate need. Fight off the desire to put your Irish setters into just any home or situation. As has been mentioned, if you are the breeder you should be, you have a strong sense of responsibility for the entire lives of these puppies. That responsibility began when you decided to let a litter be born, and continues as the puppies are dispersed.

Irish setters, as you by now know, are not for everyone. The people who come to your home may not know that and can be caught up by the cuteness of the beautiful red puppies. Your job (and you mustn't evade it) is to inform the prospective owners about Irish setter realities and responsibilities.

Your Irish Setter and Medical Care

Keeping Your Irish Setter Healthy

Preventing health problems is far less costly (and far less painful) than treating health problems. By creating a healthy environment and by having a preventive orientation you can accomplish much in the way of keeping injuries, maladies, and other unhealthy conditions away from your Irish setter. You already know about the possible hazards posed by having a large, sometimes boisterous, dog around the house. You already know about puppy-proofing your home. You already know about the need the Irish setter has for regular exercise and lots of it. You already understand the importance of a nutritionally balanced, high-quality diet.

Medical Care Team

Your Irish setter will need to have a team of concerned humans to make its good health the rule rather than the exception. On this team you will have yourself, the other members of your household, a trusted and experienced Irish setter breeder, and, of great importance—your Irish setter's veterinarian.

You and your family already have learned some accident prevention ideas. You need to learn about the most common diseases, parasites, and medical conditions that may confront your dog. You need to know how to recognize these health enemies.

Having a friend who is also really knowledgeable about Irish setters is a real bonus. This friend can be in an excellent position to monitor the well-being of your dog. Seeing the dog often enough to know it well and yet seldom enough to spot any subtle changes everyday contact might overlook, gives your expert friend a unique perspective. If you don't have such a value resource person, find one. Your dog will be better for it!

The absolutely essential member of this health team is, of course, your veterinarian. Nobody is better trained or more knowledgeable in how to keep your dog healthy than is your dog's regular

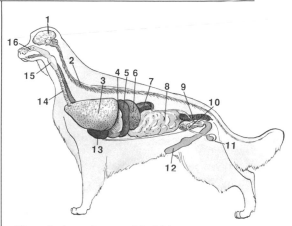

The major internal organs of the Irish setter:

1. brain	9. rectum
2. spinal cord	10. bladder
3. lungs	11. testes
4. liver	12. penis
5. stomach	13. heart
6. spleen	14. trachea
7. kidneys	15. thyroid cartilage
8. small intestine	16. sinus cavity

veterinarian. The best use of a veterinarian is not just in an emergency, but in the role of a caring professional who sees your pet on a regular basis. Establish strong rapport and clear communication with this important health giver. The veterinarian's skill and knowledge will be crucial from your dog's puppyhood to its old age.

Preventive Care for Your Irish Setter

Your in-home health care and routine visits to the veterinarian provide the basis for continuing good health for your Irish setter. The best veterinarian in the world can't help your dog if you don't take the dog to the veterinarian's office on a regular basis.

This will include visits for checkups and for vaccinations. Checkups will spot many potential problems before they become existing ones. Vacci-

Your Irish Setter and Medical Care

nations will protect your Irish setter from a number of diseases and infections. Having your dog immunized against these diseases isn't just smart, in some places it's the law!

Immunizations

Your puppy should have received its first immunizations while still under the breeder's care. The first shots include initial vaccinations for distemper, parvovirus, hepatitis, leptospirosis, parainfluenza, coronavirus, and bordetella. Your puppy should have gotten these shots at about six weeks. Follow-up shots will be necessary for most of these immunizations. Your veterinarian will set up a schedule of when these follow-ups will be needed (usually at eight to ten weeks and again at twelve weeks).

Diseases Controlled by Immunizations

Be sure your veterinarian has a complete record of all vaccinations (and other treatments) your puppy received before you got it. This is the beginning of your dog's health record, which should be kept up-to-date as long as the dog lives.

Distemper

At one time the most deadly killer of puppies and young dogs, distemper is both widespread and highly contagious. Distemper affects all the members of the canine family and a number of other small mammals. It was not uncommon a number of years ago for distemper to rage through a kennel and destroy most of the young dogs and all of the puppies.

As a viral disease, the onset of symptoms would rapidly appear about a week after exposure to an infected animal. At first, distemper would resemble a cold with a fever and a runny nose. The dog would then typically stop eating and appear tired and listless. Sometimes diarrhea would be present and the skin leathers of the nose and the pads of the feet

would thicken, which prompted old-time dog breeders to label distemper as hard pad disease.

Although some dogs would seem to recover, distemper would linger and later reappear in the form of convulsions, nervous twitching, paralysis, and death. Thankfully, vaccination has greatly decreased the incidence of occurrence of this dreadful disease.

Rabies

Rabies, or hydrophobia, was the feared "madness" that has occurred periodically since earliest time among dogs and other animals. The mere mention of the word still can conjure up terrible mental pictures of mad dogs, foaming at the mouth and running amok terrorizing a neighborhood.

Rabies is an acute infectious disease of warm-blooded mammals (including man) transmitted most commonly by an animal bite. Skunks, raccoons, bats, and foxes are among the wild animals thought to be the most common carriers of rabies. The disease still affects populations of wild animals in some parts of the world, but has been eradicated effectively in England and other countries largely by the use of strict quarantine.

Because of the fatal nature of the disease, its frightening symptoms, and the relative ease in transmission in earlier times, rabies joined the bubonic plague, leprosy, anthrax, and a few other nightmare diseases that fell eventually thanks to medicine. Louis Pasteur in 1885 developed the first vaccine against rabies. His early work, crude by modern standards, set the stage for a number of other immunizations that have made rabies a rare disease among humans (about one case a year in the United States), but a disease that should be vaccinated against in every dog.

Because your Irish setter is an active, outside dog with hunting instincts, rabies is more likely than it would be in a lap dog or sedentary pet. If your Irish setter has not been immunized and is bitten by a rabid animal, the result to the dog, and possibly even to you, can be devastating.

52

Leptospirosis

Leptospirosis is yet another canine disease that can be transmitted to humans. This bacterial disease is most commonly spread by exposure to an animal with leptospirosis or by ingestion of water that has been polluted by the urine of an infected animal. Signs of infection due to the bacteria of leptospirosis are a loss of appetite, fever, vomiting, and diarrhea. In advanced cases, serious damage to the liver and kidneys can result. Jaundice, weak hind quarters, sores in the soft tissue in the mouth, and abdominal pain are also symptoms that dogs infected with leptospirosis might evidence.

Parvovirus

A very serious ailment is parvovirus, which attacks the intestines of dogs. It is a viral disease that can mean death for many unvaccinated or untreated dogs at any time, but especially in puppies under four months of age.

Listlessness, loss of appetite followed by vomiting, and heavy, sometimes bloody diarrhea are usual parvovirus symptoms. Puppies with parvovirus can suffer from extreme dehydration. Without prompt veterinary care, death often will be the outcome. With medical care given to offset the effects of the dehydration and to handle any secondary infections, there is a reasonable chance of survival.

Parvovirus can be controlled by vaccination and common sense. Any unvaccinated dog should be viewed as a potential parvovirus victim. If your Irish setter is not vaccinated and should encounter a dog infected with parvovirus on the street or on a run at the park, you could be inviting parvovirus to infect your dog.

Hepatitis

Infectious canine hepatitis can affect a dog of any age. The severity of the disease can range from a relatively mild ailment to a fatal viral infection that can cause some dogs to die in less than a day after first observance of the symptoms.

The symptoms of hepatitis are listlessness, fever, tonsillitis, abdominal pain, vomiting, and hemorrhaging.

Parainfluenza

Often underestimated and miscalled kennel cough, parainfluenza is a highly contagious viral disease. It can spread rapidly through dogs that are housed near to one another (as in a kennel, but certainly not limited to kennels). Parainfluenza causes tracheobronchitis, which is characterized by a dry hacking cough followed by retching to expel throat mucus.

Parainfluenza, in and of itself, is not so debilitating. Untreated, however, this misnamed kennel cough can leave a dog vulnerable to more severe respiratory ailments and secondary infections. As with the other preventable diseases, parainfluenza can be prevented by vaccination. The best treatment for tracheobronchitis is provided by a veterinarian with the patient kept away from other dogs to lessen the contagion.

Coronavirus

Coronavirus is a contagious disease affecting unvaccinated dogs of various ages. Coronavirus looks very much like parvovirus. Your veterinarian will be able to distinguish coronavirus from the parvovirus.

Usually, coronavirus causes a severe diarrhea, often foul smelling, watery, and sometimes tinged with blood. The final diagnosis notwithstanding, parvovirus or coronavirus, if such symptoms are in evidence with your Irish setter, contact your veterinarian and isolate the dog until you can take it to the animal hospital.

Bordetella

Bordetella is a bacterial infection often seen in conjunction with tracheobronchitis. Your veterinarian can prevent bordetella by an immunization that will attack the whole range of the tracheobronchial infections.

Your Irish Setter and Medical Care

Lyme Disease (Spirochetosis)

Lyme disease is a serious, sometimes fatal ailment that can affect warm-blooded animals and humans. If you or your Irish setter spend any time in the fields, woods, even parks or suburban backyards where ticks abound, you should know about Lyme disease.

First recognized in the Lyme, Connecticut area, this illness is spread by the tiny deer tick. It can affect your dog in several ways; usually a swelling and tenderness in the joints is noticeable. Immediate veterinary care is essential if you even suspect that your dog has been bitten by a tick that could be a Lyme carrier.

Because the deer tick also can pass Lyme disease on to you, if you are bitten by *any* tick, you would be well advised to catch the tick and take it and yourself to your family physician, as soon as possible!

Your pet can now be protected from Lyme disease by a simple immunization from its veterinarian. You must always continue to safeguard yourself from the ticks that can bring this disease to you. If you do not find a tick, but discover what could be a tick bite surrounded by a red area, rather like a bull's eye on a target, go to your health care provider immediately. Lyme disease is yielding new information to researchers at a very rapid pace. You would be wise to keep up with developments both in the spread and treatment of this disease.

Parasites

Internal Parasites

Worms are often found in dogs and puppies and they can lead to serious health problems. Your veterinarian can discover if worms are present in your Irish setter and will prescribe an appropriate treatment. Avoid treating your dog with wormers, available from a variety of retail sources, without prior consultation with your veterinarian. Avoid any homemade worming preparations or recipes.

The veterinarian has the precise diagnostic tools to help identify parasites and modern treatments to eradicate them. Trust him or her to do it.

Regular checkups will alert you to most parasitic problems. But if you suspect that your pet may have worms, don't wait. Take your Irish setter to the veterinarian right away to make certain, and begin treatment.

Worms usually are discovered by microscopic examination of stools or a blood sample. The most common worms infecting dogs are roundworms, hookworms, tapeworms, and heartworms. Each of these must be dealt with a specific treatment approved by your veterinarian.

Roundworms: Roundworms are most often found in puppies, although dogs of any age can be infected. Puppies generally get roundworms even before they are born, if the mother dog has them.

Puppies who have roundworms simply will not thrive. Their appearance is often just not quite as sharp and shiny as uninfested puppies. They may have a pendulous abdomen, or potbelly. They may also pass worms through their stools or when they vomit. Your veterinarian can initiate elimination of the roundworms after a stool examination and a subsequent evaluation and treatment of the dog.

Clean surroundings will help eliminate these parasites. Keep the puppies' area extremely clean and sanitized; always quickly and safely dispose of any and all stools.

Hookworms: Hookworms will infect dogs of all ages, but they really will cause your puppies to do poorly. The puppies have bloody or inky stools, and do not maintain weight or eat properly. Hookworms attach themselves to the small intestines and do suck blood. Anemia can be the sometimes fatal result.

See your veterinarian promptly and keep your Irish setters away from infested areas. As with roundworms, dispose of all stools as soon as possible.

Tapeworms: Fleas are a common transmitter of tapeworms. Though they rarely debilitate a dog, these flat, segmented parasites steal from your dog's health.

Your veterinarian can treat the dog and assist you in a plan to prevent the tapeworm's return. This parasite is just another good reason for eliminating fleas from your dog's environment.

Heartworms: This wide-ranging worm is transmitted to dogs by a mosquito. The mosquito, itself infested with the heartworm larvae, passes this larvae into a dog's bloodstream and ultimately to its heart.

Because Irish setters usually spend a lot of time outdoors, heartworms can be a definite and potentially death dealing problem. If you neglect preventive treatment, it is almost certain heartworms will afflict your dog. Your veterinarian can help you with treatment that will prevent infestation. This preventative medication will help avoid the need for an expensive, possibly risky, and prolonged treatment and save your pet from an early and miserable death.

The flea can serve as host for tapeworm eggs. When a dog swallows a host flea, the tapeworm eggs are introduced into the dog's intestines to mature. Tapeworm eggs also can be found in fish or raw meat.

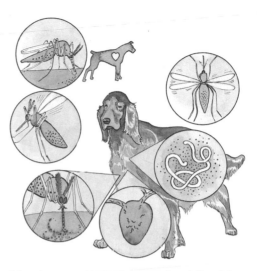

Mosquitoes spread heartworm larvae from infected dogs. The larvae mature in a dog's heart and can cause great, often fatal, damage.

External Parasites

Fleas: Fleas are the bane of many a dog's existence. They are the most common external parasite afflicting dogs. They feed on your dog's blood and in extreme cases can cause anemia. Generally they can make your Irish setter miserable. Your dog can even become infested with tapeworms transmitted by fleas.

Some Irish setters develop serious flea allergies and their coats can keep flea infestations hidden. Although fleas are bothersome to all dogs, dogs that are allergic to fleas suffer much more. Hair loss, skin problems, and incessant scratching may indicate this allergy. Prompt treatment by a veterinarian can do much to alleviate this uncomfortable condition.

Dealing with fleas involves a warfare mentality—a them-or-us kind of thinking. You have to hit fleas at *every* phase of their existence in order to achieve even a limited victory. Everywhere a dog with fleas has been will have fleas—the bed, the

Your Irish Setter and Medical Care

yard, the doghouse, the car, your house. If you fail to attack the fleas in *any* of these areas, then you have failed—the fleas will be back.

Flea dips, flea shampoos, flea powder, flea collars, and flea sprays are all designed for use on dogs. Consult your veterinarian about these. Be sure to treat the dog's den and its bedding. Flea foggers will provide some relief for your home. In severe cases, you may need to call your exterminator. Fleas spend only about 10 percent of their time on the dog. That means that 90 percent of the time fleas are available to visit your home, yard, and so on.

There are yard sprays for the outside areas where your Irish setter lives. Always be careful in their use. For more serious infestations, consult a professional exterminator.

Ticks: As a dog that spends a lot of time outside, your Irish setter can come in contact with another vicious blood sucker, the tick. Ticks live in the woods, at the park, and even in your own yard. Although regular dips will control ticks rather well, you need to know how to handle them if you see them.

Ticks are much larger than fleas and as they become engorged on blood they can get as big as a marble if left in place. Never simply pull a tick off your dog. You will leave part of its mouth parts in the dog. The best way to get rid of these suckers is to place a drop of alcohol at the location where the tick is attached to the skin. Let the alcohol cause the tick to loosen its grip a bit. Using tweezers, grasp the tick as close to the dog's skin as possible and pull slowly. Be sure to get the mouth of the tick when you pull the pest away. Put alcohol on the bite and dispose of the tick carefully (they can get back on the dog or on you if simply dropped on the ground).

Ticks have gained recent notoriety with the discovery of Lyme disease (see page 54) in dogs and in humans. This potentially life-threatening disease is transmitted by the deer tick, and has been found in many areas across the United States. If a tick bites you, keep it and see a medical professional immediately to identify it. Regular dipping and careful checks after all treks into areas where ticks may live will help you and your Irish setter remain tick free.

Ear Mites: Ear mites can cause your Irish setter great discomfort. These microscopic mites live in the ear canal. Their presence can cause the development of a dark waxy residue. They can be easily transmitted to and from other dogs (or cats). Symptoms include shaking of the head from side to side and increased ear scratching. Your veterinarian can identify and treat them quickly and effectively.

Mange: Another problem brought to the dog by mites is mange. There are two kinds: red mange (or demodectic) and scabies (or sarcoptic).

Red mange especially affects old dogs and young puppies and causes scruffy hair loss and other symptoms. It varies in degree of severity from dog to dog. Itching may sometimes accompany red mange. Seek help immediately. Don't mess around with mange.

Scabies mites also burrow into the dog's epidermal skin layer. They are highly contagious and can spread from your dog to other dogs or to you. Sarcoptic mange causes really unsightly hair loss and a lot of itching. See your veterinarian immediately for proper diagnosis and treatment.

Other Skin Problems: Like other dog breeds, Irish setters are sometimes beset with any of a number of skin problems—allergies, fungi, and so on. Flea bite allergy is one skin problem that stems directly from an allergic reaction to fleas (see page 55). Some dogs may develop allergies to certain foods or to some other aspect of their environments. Some dogs are born with genetically carried problems. Your veterinarian usually can pinpoint the sources of these conditions and help in either preventing the problem or in dealing with it.

Rely on your veterinarian in diagnosing and treating skin problems. Home remedies here can often make a condition much worse. Let a professional, with all the information and resources available, develop the treatment plan for your dog. You won't regret it—nor will your pet.

Your Irish Setter and Medical Care

Common Illnesses and Medical Problems

Vomiting and Diarrhea

Some vomiting and diarrhea is the result of normal things like dietetic changes or stress. In puppies, vomiting and diarrhea are most commonly caused by intestinal parasites. Both are possible indicators of other more serious conditions. Any prolonged vomiting or diarrhea deserves at least a call to the veterinarian's office. Early treatment is effective treatment. Until you have gained more experience, take care in all such situations.

If either vomiting or diarrhea becomes severe or continues for more than 12 to 24 hours, you would be wise to take your Irish setter to your veterinarian.

Constipation

If normal bowel movements have not been occurring for your Irish setter or if the dog is clearly straining to defecate, constipation may be the cause. Many dietetic causes, like eating bones or a sudden change in dog food, can bring on constipation. Sometimes a dog that has been traveling and not allowed relief walks on a regular basis will become constipated.

Usually constipation is a minor problem, but check with your veterinarian if it continues, especially if the dog is in obvious pain and crying out while trying to defecate.

Impacted Anal Sacs

The anal sacs lie just under the skin on each side of the anus. Normally these are emptied of their strong-smelling secretions during defecation. Sometimes however, they become clogged (impacted) and must be emptied by hand. Your veterinarian can show you how to do this. When you see a dog scooting along the floor or ground dragging its rear end, impacted anal sacs or possible tapeworm irritation could be the cause.

Gastic Tortion or Bloat

Bloat is an extremely serious problem that tends to strike dogs of the larger, deep-chested breeds. Irish setters have been known to be affected by this condition.

Bloat has been associated with the overfeeding of dry dog food followed by a large intake of water and vigorous exercise. Bloat tends to affect males more than females and often its victims are over twenty-four months of age. Some scientists believe that a genetic predisposition to bloat may exist within certain breeds and even within certain families within these breeds.

Bloat involves the swelling of a dog's stomach from gas or from water or perhaps these two in combination. The symptoms are:
• obvious abdominal pain and noticeable swelling;
• excessive salivation and rapid breathing; and
• pale and cool-to-the-touch skin in the mouth and gums; the dog looks dazed and in shock.

If your dog begins to exhibit these symptoms after a large meal followed by heavy exercise, don't wait around. *Rush this dog to the nearest veterinarian!* Death from bloat can be sudden.

Hip Dysplasia

Hip dysplasia is an all too common inheritable ailment that seems to, like bloat, affect larger breed dogs especially. It is the major cause of lameness in the hindquarters of dogs. In hip dysplasia, there is a defect in the formation of the hip joint itself. This is a very sad condition to affect your pet; walking becomes increasingly painful.

This is one of the most important items to check before you buy a puppy. You would be very wise (especially if you believe you want to raise Irish setters) to insist that your puppy's parents both have OFA (Orthopedic Foundation for Animals) certification numbers showing they have been x-rayed and found to have normal hips. Your puppy cannot be checked by x-ray until it is two years old.

Progressive Retinal Atrophy (PRA)

This condition was actually first recognized in Irish setters, but now appears to affect a number of other breeds of all sizes and types. PRA is a degenerative disease that generally affects mature to older dogs. It attacks the cells of the retina, first causing night blindness and leading to a complete loss of sight.

PRA has been shown to be an inherited condition. As with hip dysplasia, you must certainly avoid an Irish setter puppy with PRA in its pedigree. Check with the Irish Setter Club of America to learn about PRA-free breeders in your area.

Emergency Care

Poisoning

Protecting your Irish setter puppy from some toxic products and conditions has been discussed. There are other accidental poisoning possibilities to be known about that generally will require immediate veterinary care.

Antifreeze is highly poisonous but has an odor and taste that attracts dogs. A number of house and yard plants are deadly if eaten. Chocolate can be poisonous to most dogs. Some insect bites or stings can have strong negative reactions for your Irish setter.

Because Irish setters are often outdoor sporting dogs, the range of poisons that possibly can be encountered increases. Everything from poisons put out for predators to poisonous snakebites can threaten an outside dog. Your veterinarian is, as always, your best source of treatment and preventative information.

Be alert to listlessness, convulsions, disoriented behavior, vomiting, diarrhea, and a change in the color of mucus membranes. Get your pet to the veterinarian as soon as possible.

Accidents

Many accidents can be prevented by just thinking ahead and being a little creatively paranoid

An injured dog can hurt itself or you. Using care and tenderness, fashion a makeshift muzzle from a belt or other available item before attempting to move the animal.

about things that can hurt your dog. But as careful as you are, accidents can still happen.

If your dog has been injured, be careful not to make the injury worse or to be bitten by a dog in pain. Using a piece of cloth (a necktie or handkerchief will do) as a muzzle, gently lift your Irish setter and place it on a makeshift stretcher made of your shirt, a towel, or some other cloth that will allow you to move the injured dog without danger of further injury. Call the veterinarian to alert him or her to the situation and drive safely there.

One way to help your Irish setter stay uninjured is not to let it range freely. Irish setters, like many large, sporting breeds, love to run. Unfortunately, their running can take them into the paths of automobiles. Death or severe injury is often the result of a collision between a lovely but heedless Irish setter and a car.

Bleeding

If your Irish setter appears to be bleeding, identify the source of the blood and apply firm but gentle pressure to the area. If the injury is on an extremity, place a tourniquet between the wound and the heart, but it must be loosened for 30 to 60 seconds every 15 minutes. Continued bleeding or any significant blood loss or a gaping wound will require veterinarian attention. Treat any bleeding as a serious condition.

Heatstroke

A healthy, happy Irish setter can be dying or dead in just a few minutes in a car with poor ventilation and high inside temperature. Just a few minutes in the sun on even a moderately warm day—60°F (15.6°C) or so—even with some windows partially rolled down, can mean the dog's death.

Never take chances with your dog in an enclosed area. It can be fatal to your pet.

Heatstroke symptoms include a dazed look and rapid, shallow panting with a high fever. The dog's gums will be bright red. This is one situation where you must act before going to the veterinarian. Immediately lower the dog's temperature by applying cool water or a mixture of cool water and alcohol externally administered. Rush it immediately to the *nearest* veterinary hospital.

Old Age and Your Irish Setter

Aging is a natural process that will affect both you and your Irish setter. The bouncy puppy will give way to the young adult who will become the mature dog who will become your long-time companion and old friend. Irish setters normally have a long life span, especially for a larger breed, but aging is not without its adjustments. As your dog begins to reach eight or nine years of age (some dogs age more quickly than others), certain changes will become evident. Your Irish setter may begin to slow down a little, sleep more, and generally be less active.

Your dog may begin to experience certain age-related health problems with its teeth and gums, bowels and bladder, eyesight and hearing. Your good preventive care that began in puppyhood, along with regular veterinarian visits, can forestall or delay many of these concerns, but if your Irish setter lives long enough, some age-related problems will present themselves.

Health Areas to Watch

Teeth

Throughout the life of your Irish setter, tartar buildup on its teeth will be a problem. Feeding a premium quality dry dog food will serve as an abrasive to help keep your Irish setter's teeth clean. Chew toys, nylon bones, dog biscuits, and similar products also will help, but brushing from puppyhood on will help keep down plaque and tartar. If you pay attention to your dog's teeth early on and then consistently thereafter, your dog will have nicer teeth and fresher breath.

If you will utilize one of the new canine oral care kits (a toothbrush and toothpaste) on a regular basis, your pet will have a much better chance to avoid dental problems later on. Weak, loose, or decayed teeth and gum problems can plague older dogs and cause other health problems. You could have your veterinarian begin early in your pup's life to clean its teeth. Check your dog's teeth on a weekly basis. Don't neglect your Irish setter's choppers. You'll regret it if you do.

Eyes

Eye care, under normal conditions, is not a major problem. Always use good preventive measures, such as avoiding any sharp objects at eye level that might harm your Irish setter, as a part of your adult dog-proofing of the kennel, yard, and home.

Your Irish Setter and Medical Care

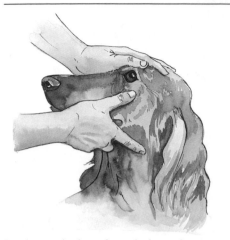

Regular examinations of your dog's eyes by you or your veterinarian can detect any problems or injuries that may require further attention.

You may on occasion see some mucus-like matter collecting in the corners of your dog's eyes. This is of no real consequence. Use a tissue and gently wipe the material out of the eyes.

As with other medical matters, use common sense. If your dog begins to have excessive eye discharge, redness, or evident discomfort, consult your veterinarian. As with humans, dogs can suffer from exposure to chemical fumes (household cleaners, exterminators) or from smoke (cigarette or fireplace). An Irish setter that goes afield often may run into eye-threatening conditions or circumstances. After such activities, always check your dog's eyes for any injuries.

Older dogs sometimes develop cataracts, an opaqueness of the lens. You will notice a gradual clouding of the eye. Cataracts can be part of the aging process. Other than the cosmetic aspects and some vision impairment, cataracts usually are not serious. (For another age-related eye problem, see PRA on page 58.)

Ears

Much of the regular observation you do to guard against ear mites will help you monitor overall ear health. Your veterinarian also will help you prevent problems here. If the ears begin to show inflammation or the dog repeatedly is bothered with its ears, there may be an infection. Don't delay in seeking professional care.

After your Irish setter has had access to any wooded area, you should always remember that the ears are a favorite target area for ticks. Always check for these critters if your setter has been where ticks may be lurking.

Nails

Part of a consistent care regimen for your dog will be regular attention to its toenails. Beginning while your Irish setter is still a puppy, its nails should be kept trimmed. Starting early and gently, your pet will not fear nail trimming, which it will need on a regular basis for the rest of its life. Failure to keep the nails at an appropriate length can result in pain for your Irish setter. Even if your dog runs on sidewalks or other surfaces that can help keep the nail worn down, regular checks by you will be necessary.

When trimming your Irish setter's nails, avoid cutting into the "quick" or part of the nail that will bleed. Your veterinarian can show you how to do it correctly.

How to Administer Medicine

Although much of your pet's health care will rest in the hands of your veterinarian, being able to administer the prescription medicines is good to know. Your Irish setter may not like taking medicine and may spit out pills and capsules. One way to get pills, like monthly heartworm medication, into the dog is by hiding them in some treat item. One dog breeder used a small piece of bread smeared with smooth peanut butter to make the medicine go down.

The direct approach is simply to open your Irish setter's mouth, tilting the head back just a little way and placing the pill as far back on the tongue as you can. Close the dog's mouth and wait for it to swallow. *It is important not to just casually toss the pill into the dog's mouth or tilt the head back too far, or the pill could be caught in the windpipe instead of going down the throat.* Liquid medicine is administered in a similar way by tilting the head back only slightly and pouring the liquid dosage into the back of the dog's mouth. Tilting the head too far back also can cause possible choking as the liquid may flow into the windpipe.

Euthanasia

One of the saddest moments in a dog owner's life comes with the realization that age, infirmity, or terminal illness has made life for the pet a painful, negative experience. Your Irish setter, unless taken prematurely by illness or accident, will grow to be a very old dog. That red flash that used to run rapidly ahead of you on outings gradually will slow down

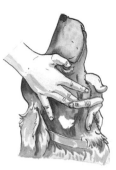

After administering medicine, close the mouth and tilt the head back only slightly to avoid a pill from possibly being caught in your dog's windpipe. Rub its neck to encourage swallowing.

until the once quick youngster becomes the now trailing oldster valiantly struggling to keep up.

It is never easy to bid farewell to a friend and pet whose life has meant so much to yours. It may not be easy, but it certainly is preferable to watching this companion live in constant pain, unable to go about even the most basic daily activities.

Your veterinarian will, by now, also be an old friend of your Irish setter. Talk with the veterinarian and discuss the option of alleviating your pet's misery. Euthanasia, although a painful decision for you, is a painless procedure for your aging Irish setter. It is also a great kindness for an animal who isn't able to philosophically understand why old age hurts so much. When your Irish setter can no longer experience the joy of living, your decision should be a clear if not easy one to make.

Training Your Irish Setter

Your puppy's mother already has begun to teach it "pack" behavior. By understanding and using this canine methodology, you can make training your puppy much simpler.

The Key to Training— Understanding Pack Behavior

Your adorable red puppy is a pack animal just like the wolf, the sled dog, or the foxhound. Pack behavior is a natural, integral part of your Irish setter and, as such, is the key to training it to be a good canine companion and citizen.

The pack, quite simply, is a canine caste system where each member has, and knows it has, a place. The pack system provides security and a sense of belonging that is crucial to a well-adjusted dog. A dog's position in the pack hierarchy usually is based on physical strength and experience—the strongest male with the most savvy fills the role of alpha or first male.

The alpha dog leads the pack. He resolves differences between pack members, imposes his will on the pack, and helps guide and teach the young or inexperienced in what is expected of them as pack

members. He remains the alpha dog only as long as he is the strongest.

You will have to fill this role for your Irish setter and your family will have to serve as the pack .members. Your puppy will have learned some pack behavior by its mother and littermates. You and the other members of your household will be a logical (and necessary) extension of what your puppy has learned from its mother.

Training will be much easier if you follow the example of your dog's mother. She taught it, almost from the moment of its birth, the things it would

Top: Grooming can be an enjoyable experience for you ▶ and your Irish setter.
Bottom: In addition to prompt attention when your dog seems ill, regular visits to the veterinarian are essential for your dog's good health.

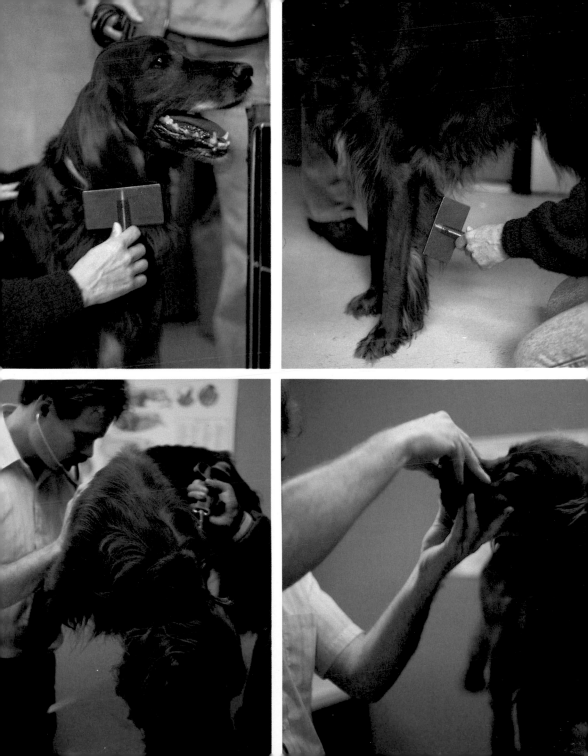

need to survive. As the pup matured, she reprimanded it, loved it, and taught it in a way that you can and should follow:

• She admonished the puppy *immediately* for any misdeeds (while the puppy, with its short attention span, could identify action with outcome).

• She *fairly* corrected the puppy, neither overreacting to nor ignoring its mistake.

• She dealt with the puppy in a *consistent* manner. The same behavior did not get a loving lick one time and a warning growl the next.

• There was *no anger* in her training. Her reprimand wasn't savage nor did she bark at it endlessly in an effort to "verbalize" the puppy into correct behavior.

• She reprimanded the puppy with *love* and made it feel secure, even if it had done something that had warranted correction earlier in the day. She didn't withhold love to force the puppy to act correctly.

The mother dog's lessons to the puppy have much to teach us about training. Not only does your puppy already understand these lessons, but the lessons worked for her and will work for you!

When you take your puppy away from its mother and the security of the litterpack, you immediately should move to fill this gap. You and your family should work to understand the role of the pack in the emotional well-being of your Irish setter. You (or your designated person) must become the alpha dog to help this puppy learn its lessons. Your Irish setter will want to please you, but it must know that you love it and will care for it. How your red puppy goes about learning what it must do to please you is up to you. One thing is certain, the puppy won't learn these lessons by simple osmosis, it must be trained.

◀ Although Irish setters can adapt to living in an apartment or small house, daily outings to a park or field where your pet can run to its heart's content will help keep your dog in top condition—and in good spirits!

When to Begin Training

Housebreaking and basic rules can begin immediately after you get the puppy settled in. More involved training should begin between five and eight months based on your dog's own level of maturity. Some pups are ready earlier than others.

Essentials of Training

• You and your puppy will need a regularly set time (perhaps a couple of times a day) free from distractions (other dogs, running children). This time should be short (not more than 15 minutes) and, although enjoyable, it should be work time, not playtime.

• You need to have a clear idea (perhaps discussed with other members of your family) of what you want your Irish setter to learn. Consistency is important. You can't be correcting behavior that everyone else in the family ignores or even rewards!

• You are the boss, the alpha dog. Use a stern tone of voice during the training sessions to differentiate from other times when you and the Irish setter are together. Although this is an authoritarian's hat, it is not a drill sergeant's hat. These sessions should never be conducted when you are angry at the dog, your spouse, or your boss. Your anger or frustration will come through and intimidate your puppy.

• Each session should be conducted as a class. The pup's learning is the objective. If the command "come" is to be taught today, don't try to go over the variations of "fetch" or "roll over." Stick to the subject. Review previous lessons and praise the dog when it does something right. Correct *each* time it doesn't do what it should, but make sure that the dog understands what you want. If you can't get a lesson across, go back to something the dog does well. Do that several times, praise the dog, and stop for the day.

• Use appropriate praise for a successful action. This doesn't mean if the dog does what you want one time you roughhouse for the rest of the time. Reward with praise effectively, but save play for

later (allow a few minutes of lag time between the lesson and the playtime so that the two are not confused).
• As the mother dog would do, correct misdeeds immediately while you help the puppy to identify the behavior or error with your correction. Don't attempt to punish a dog for something done some time ago. It won't remember or understand or know why you are correcting it (free-floating reprimands don't do anything but confuse the dog when you do want to change its behavior).
• Always be patient and never become angry. Ranting and raving or physically punishing the dog can destroy your puppy's trust in you. A simple, firm "no" will suffice. Remember the lack of temper the mother dog used with her puppies.

Housebreaking

You already have begun to help your Irish setter learn in this area. Your puppy will want to please you, but it also will have the basic need to eliminate wastes. Your task is to help the puppy learn how to please you by eliminating its wastes at a certain place and time of your choosing.

No matter how much your Irish setter puppy may want to please you, it will have limited bladder control until somewhere between four and six months of age. Until this age, don't expect complete housebreaking to take place. That does not mean that you don't provide a solid foundation for the time when the dog's physical functioning catches up with its desire to please you.

Crate training takes advantage of the dog's innate desire to keep its den clean. (See Crate Training Hints, page 67.) It is also an excellent way to help housebreak your puppy. Crate training does, however, require a regular plan for feeding and for visits outside. When crate training is combined with this plan and a good deal of praise when the puppy does what you want, it will work exceptionally well.

You have, with your family, decided how much time you will want your Irish setter to stay inside with you. Regardless of this amount of time, if your Irish setter is to be in your home at all, it will need to be housebroken.

Some basic understanding of when your puppy will need to relieve itself is essential. Take the puppy out to the established relief area after it eats or drinks (additional food causes additional pressure on the colon and bladder). Go out first thing each morning and after naps during the day. Go out after a long, strenuous play session. Go out as late at night as possible. By all means, take the pup out if it begins to show signs of wanting to defecate or urinate—staying near the door, circling, and sniffing with a general uneasy look.

Sometimes you will get the puppy outside just in time. When the puppy relieves itself in the appropriate place, praise it immediately. Stay with the puppy until it does eliminate and you have rewarded it with praise. Help the puppy learn the behavior you expect of it. Never scold the dog at the appointed elimination location; give positive reinforcement at this all important site. Don't confuse your Irish setter by sending mixed messages.

Never strike the puppy if it has an accident. A firm "No" will let the puppy know the displeasure that the action merits. *Never* rub the puppy's nose in urine or excrement. This not only will discourage positive behavior, but then you have to clean up the puppy. In letting your puppy know what is bad behavior and by praising good behavior, you highlight the rewarded act and make it the memorable thing.

Feeding your Irish setter at regular times will help you anticipate when the puppy needs to go out. Using a premium dog food will produce much firmer stools with less volume, which will be easier to clean up if a mess does happen. Never feed table scraps as treats. They will only upset the nutritional balance of the quality food. Do not leave food out for your puppy all day. Your Irish setter puppy will do well on three to four meals a day.

By its very nature, your puppy will not want to soil its den. Its mother gave it firm, early lessons in keeping the whelping box, your puppy's first home, clean. Use this innate behavior combined with regular meals and regular walks; you will help the puppy win your praise and avoid the stern "No" that comes from making a mess.

Even though crate training is probably the most efficient and effective way to housebreak your puppy, it may not work out for those who cannot be at home with their puppy during those first few days of adjustment. For these people, paper training (a slower, but still effective method) can be used.

Paper training involves confining the puppy to some easily cleaned area (a kitchen, a bathroom, or a laundry room). Paper training does not work overly well with outside training because the puppy is given two "right" places to go. Paper training, however, may be necessary for those whose schedules cannot revolve around the puppy. It also is helpful for those who live in multistoried apartments and others to whom quick trips outside are not accomplished easily. (Note: Although there are certainly some Irish setters in such an enclosed environment, most breed experts would prefer to see the big red dogs in a setting offering more opportunity for the high level of exercise that Irish setters need.)

Three areas in the puppy's space are needed: the elimination area, the food and water area, and the den area containing the carrier/crate/cage. The area set aside for elimination should be covered with several layers of black and white newspapers. The puppy is urged to use this part of the room, the part with the newspapers. Praise is given every time the puppy does what it is supposed to do in the right area. Most dogs do not like to soil either their sleeping areas or their eating areas; neither should be too close to the papered area. When the pup uses the waste area, the top paper is removed. The puppy's scent remains on the lower layers. This encourages the puppy to use the paper again when it needs to relieve itself.

By using the paper training method, housebreaking will take a little longer. Even with paper

training, be sure to walk your puppy early each morning and late each night. You cannot completely keep from taking the puppy outside. Gradually decrease the size of the area covered by newspaper until only a small part of the room is used for relief. Some advocate taking that small section of paper outside with you to let the pup use it there in the later stages of training, which centers on shifting the puppy from the paper to a location outside.

The use of the crate by your puppy gives you the extra bonus of being able to regulate the puppy's access to things that might do it harm when you are not around to care for it. Such use for an Irish setter not only is humane but in keeping with the nature of the species. As your pup matures, it will continue to have the crate as its own place within its environment.

If your puppy does make a mistake, get that area cleaned up quickly. Use an odor-removing cleaner. If the puppy should happen on the area where its scent indicates it has relieved itself, it may do so again. If your puppy has inordinate difficulty either with defecation or urination, there may be some medical issue that will require a visit to the veterinarian.

If you live in an urban area and your puppy must use a public street or sidewalk as its elimination area, curb your dog; pick up and properly dispose of any excreta. Being a responsible dog owner is being a good dog owner. The responsibility is yours; many urban laws require you to clean up after your pet.

Crate Training Hints

• Keep a positive attitude about crates/cages/carriers and the positive role they can play in providing a den for your Irish setter.
• Be sure to buy a large enough crate/cage/carrier to comfortably serve as a den for your Irish setter when it is an adult. Make a movable, temporary partition to keep the den just the right size as your puppy matures.

Training Your Irish Setter

Crate training your Irish setter is not a cruel or heartless action. It utilizes natural canine instincts and can aid greatly aid in housebreaking your puppy.

• Place the den in an out-of-the-way, but not isolated, part of the household always in use but out of any temperature fluctuations that could make it uncomfortable at times.
• Put the puppy in the crate/cage/carrier for naps and when it must be left unattended for several hours. When you return, immediately take the puppy outside to the elimination location. Praise the puppy when it defecates or urinates, pick up the puppy and go right back inside the house.
• Use a stern alpha-leader, authoritative voice to quiet any whining or barking of the pup when being placed in the den.
• Do not praise the puppy for about 10 minutes after is it let out of the cage/crate/carrier. To do so will make getting out more of a reward than you want it to be.
• During training, put the puppy back in the den after about 30 minutes outside of it and make the puppy quiet down.
• Keep a mat or towel in the den along with a favorite chew to make it a comfortable place.
• Do not put food or water in the crate/cage/carrier. Food and water have their place outside the crate.
• Make sure your family and frequent visitors to your house fully understand the importance of crate training and why and how it must be done.

Basic Training

When your Irish setter is about five or six months old, it usually is mature enough to learn the basic obedience commands that will make it a better pet and companion. Unfortunately some dog owners fail to give their pets the advantages of training. For an active dog like an Irish setter, this is a real shame. Not only will the breed's natural rollicking nature tend to be more of a problem than an asset, but the dog never will get an opportunity to become the pet it has the potential to be. These people and their dogs miss out on one of the great joys of human-canine interaction—the ability of the human to find a way to communicate with the canine and shape the canine's behavior, having a good time in the process.

Training Equipment

You will need a chain training collar of the type commonly called a choke-chain. This is the most effective and humane way to train your puppy. When you use this collar correctly the collar does not choke the dog, it merely provides a restraining, correcting pressure when given a quick tug upward. This gets the pup's attention and also serves as a correcting method. The quick tug and the stern word, "No," let the puppy know it has done wrong. The collar will need to be large enough to go over your Irish setter puppy's head at it widest part with about one inch to spare but not much more. A choke-chain collar generally is used for training only. Before beginning each lesson, swap your puppy's regular collar (the one attached to its personal identification and rabies vaccination tags) for the training collar.

With the training collar you will need a ¾- to 1-inch (2.2–2.5 cm) wide leash (or lead) measuring about 6 feet (1.8 m) long. The lead can be leather, web, or nylon. The lead will need to have a swivel snap at one end for fastening through the ring on the training collar. At the other end, the lead should have a comfortable hand loop. This lead is, of course, longer than your normal walking leash.

Carefully familiarize your puppy with the training collar and with the lead so that the puppy will not come to fear or loath either. In a large room or open area outside where there are no obstacles to snag the lead, let your pup run around with the training collar on and the lead trailing along behind. This gives the puppy the feel of the weight of the collar and lead before training time actually begins.

Issue clear, one-word commands to your dog, such as "Sit." Use the dog's name before each command and be authoritarian in your tone. Use the same tone each time. Don't confuse your dog by using two commands at one time, such as "Sit, down." Also remember the canine learning rules: praise enthusiastically; correct fairly and immediately; practice consistent repetition; and don't lose your temper.

The Five Basic Commands

Sit

The "sit" is a good common command on which to start a puppy. Your pup already knows how to sit, all you need to do is to teach it when and where to do so. With the training collar attached to the lead, place your puppy on your left side next to your left leg, while holding the lead in your right hand. In one continuous, gentle motion, pull the pup's head up as you push its hindquarters down with your left hand giving the firm command, "Sit" as you do so.

When the pup is in the sitting position, lavishly praise it. Using the concept of consistent repetition, repeat the lesson until your pup sits down without its rear end being pushed downward. Remember to keep the same upward pressure on the lead to prevent a "sit" from becoming a belly flop. If the dog shifts in position left or right, use your left hand to move it back to where it belongs. Keep doing this exercise until the Irish setter associates the word "sit" and your tone with the praise it will receive if it sits down. Soon the puppy will sit upon hearing

As the "sit" command is given, press gently on the dog's hindquarters with your left hand while gently pulling up on the lead with the right hand.

the word alone without the rear end push or the raised lead. Always use praise liberally. Make the praise and the lesson stick out in your puppy's memory.

Keep training time brief. Initially don't leave the young dog in the sitting position long enough to bore it. Gradually increase the time for sitting. Remember, consistent repetition with praise and correction will help your pup learn. You may have to begin all over again for a while. Your pup will learn more quickly with several brief, consistent sessions than with one long session.

Stay

Do not attempt to teach "stay" until your pup has mastered "sit." The stay is begun from the sit and without that foundation, the stay cannot be learned.

To begin the stay command, you place your dog in a regular sitting position on your left. Keep some pressure on the lead in your right hand to keep the puppy's head up. Giving the clear, authoritative command, "Stay," you step away from the dog

"Stay" begins with your dog in a "sit." Give the command "Stay" while stepping away from the dog (right foot first) and bringing the palm of your left hand down and in front of the dog's face.

Each time the pup obeys the stay command, praise it. You will be able to gradually move further away and the puppy will eventually get the idea. Introduce the release word "okay" in a cheerful, happy way when you want to let the puppy know that it now can come to you and be praised.

Because of the conflicts the puppy feels—wanting to please you and wanting to be with you—the stay is fairly difficult, but with patience and consistency you will see your Irish setter master it.

Heel

Now that your puppy feels comfortable with the training collar and lead, you can teach it to "heel." Begin teaching the heel command with the Irish setter on your left side, its head next to your left foot, in the sit position. Holding the lead in your right hand and leading with your left foot, step forward, saying in a firm, authoritative alpha voice, "Heel." Use the dog's name to begin the command, as in, "Russ, heel." If your pup doesn't move out when you do, snap the lead sharply against your leg and repeat the command, walking away as you do. As soon as your puppy catches up with you, praise it but keep moving. Continue using praise and encouragement as long as it stays with you in proper position.

When you stop, tell your dog to sit. As the Irish setter becomes more accustomed to heeling, it will learn to sit on its own when you stop. Don't let your dog lag behind or run ahead or edge around to face you. The purpose of the "heel" command is not just to walk your dog but to position the dog on your left and teach it to move and stop when you move and stop. The ultimate goal of heeling would be to have the dog do this without the use of the lead.

Never drag your puppy with you just to cover some ground. Go back to sit and begin the command again. The heel command is tough for some dogs to learn. Continue your use of tugs on the lead to keep your puppy moving and keep its head in line with your left leg. Irish setters are bright and most can learn heeling in a few consistent, patient lessons.

(moving your right foot first). At the same time, you bring the palm of your left hand down in front of your Irish setter's face. Your command, the stepping away (moving the right foot first), and the hand signal must be done simultaneously and in exactly the same way each time.

Maintain eye contact with your dog and repeat the "stay" command (in the same firm tone as before). Don't really expect long stays in the beginning. Praise the puppy for its stays whatever their length, but if it moves toward you, take it back to the starting point, make it sit, and begin again with consistent repetition. Patience is crucial. Your puppy loves you and wants to come to you. If your pup has trouble with the stay, don't tire it out by attempting the command over and over again. Go back to the sit (a command which the puppy can do well) and enthusiastically praise your Irish setter when it sits correctly.

The "heel" command also begins with the "sit." Placing the lead in your right hand, teach the dog to walk on your left.

Down

"Down" begins with the "sit" and the "stay." Using the lead in an opposite movement from the upward pressure used with the sit and the stay, pull down on the lead with your right hand, presenting the palm of your left hand with a downward motion while clearly giving the command, "Down." If the dog doesn't want to lie down, run the lead under your left foot and pull up on it gently, which will pull the pup's head downward. Repeat the hand signal and the command, "Down." Once the pup is in the down position, pour on the praise. You can help your pup in the beginning by using your left hand, as in the sit command, but pushing on the back rather than on the hindquarters. It is the downward direction that this command emphasizes, but it also should be used in conjunction with the stay. The ultimate goal is to cause the puppy to go straight down on its stomach and remain there until released by an "okay" command from you.

The down is a very useful and important command and can be used to stop your Irish setter in its tracks when it might be heading for trouble or danger. Practice the down with the sit and the stay and make sure that your puppy is lavishly rewarded when it stays put in the down position. By consistent repetition, you should be able to gradually increase the length of the down and even leave the Irish setter's presence and expect it to remain in place. As with the stay, your dog should not move about. Correct it if it does, praise it if it doesn't.

Come

The "come" command may seem obvious and easy, but there are several key elements to it. Enthusiasm and use of the dog's name and the command with wide open arms will let the puppy know you really want to be with it. This seems like a natural behavior, yet so many people foolishly call their dogs and then scold, punish, or even whip them. To an intelligent Irish setter puppy the command, "Come" by you (or any of your family) if followed by a reprimand could cause this natural behavior to be unlearned quickly. *Never* call your dog to you to correct or punish it. If the dog must be corrected, you go to the dog and do it.

Always use lots of praise on the puppy when it comes at your call. Remember that the dog must learn that "come," like the other commands, must be obeyed immediately and each and every time. If your dog is a little stubborn or inattentive to the command, give the lead (which of course is still in use) a firm but gentle tug to get movement in your direction started. This method will work, especially when combined with the authoritative command from you as the alpha leader and the warm tones and friendly gesturing that follow it. If not, a little sharper tug used with the command can be used. You have your puppy on a 6-foot (1.8 m) lead but a longer lead can be used—up to 20 feet (6 m)—to reinforce the command from a greater distance.

One point in the come command is different from the other commands. It does not need to be

"Come" is a command that is best taught with the use of a long lead. Remember *never* to call the dog to you to punish it. This results in unlearning of the "come" command.

repeated over and over again during a lesson. Use it when you are working on the other lessons or when your dog is involved in play or something else.

Always expect the dog to obey this command quickly and praise the dog when it complies.

Remember that using "come" and then reprimanding is a way to untrain your dog. Make sure that each member of your family understands this. In discussing this with your family, let each person learn all the different commands and the correct "hows" and "whys" of each part. This will make things much saner for your puppy, who can't possibly learn when it is getting conflicting usages of the same word from different members of its "pack."

Obedience Classes

If, for whatever reason, you can't seem to teach your Irish setter, don't hesitate to enlist the help of a professionally run obedience school or class. Sometimes there is a local dog club where obedience lessons are offered. Much of what will be taught in these classes will help you train yourself to train your dog. There are many other things that a smart Irish setter can learn beyond these basic commands discussed. You may want to give your pup (or adult dog) a chance at higher education if it seems to have the aptitude and you want to try it.

Useful Addresses and Literature

International Kennel Clubs

Irish Setter Club of America*
  Mrs. Joyce Mumford
  Recording Secretary
  12318 Highway 62
  Charlestown, Indiana 47111

The National Red Setter Field Trial Club
  Bob Sprouse, Secretary
  Rt. 1, Box 72B
  Cypress Inn, Tennessee 38452

American Kennel Club
  51 Madison Avenue
  New York, New York 10038

Australian National Kennel Club
  Royal Show Ground
  Ascot Vale
  Victoria, Australia

Canadian Kennel Club
  2150 Bloor Street West
  Toronto, Ontario M6540
  Canada

Irish Kennel Club
  41 Harcourt Street
  Dublin 2
  Ireland

The Kennel Club
  1-4 Clargis Street
  Picadilly
  London, W7Y 8AB
  England

New Zealand Kennel Club
  P.O. Box 523
  Wellington, 1
  New Zealand

*This address may change as a new officer is elected. The very latest listing always can be obtained from the American Kennel Club.

Information and Printed Materials

American Boarding Kennel Association
  4575 Galley Road, Suite 400A
  Colorado Springs, Colorado 80915
  (Publishes lists of approved kennels.)

American Society for the Prevention of Cruelty to Animals (ASPCA)
  441 East 92nd Street
  New York, New York 10028

American Veterinary Medical Association
  930 North Meacham Road
  Schaumburg, Illinois 60173

Gaines TWT
  P.O. Box 8172
  Kankakee, Illinois 60901
  (Publishes "Touring with Towser," a directory of hotels and motels that accommodate guests with dogs.)

Humane Society of the United States
  2100 L Street N.W.
  Washington, DC 20037

Books

In addition to the most recent edition of the official publication of the American Kennel Club, *The Complete Dog Book*, published by Howell House, Inc., New York, other suggestions include:

Alderton, David. *The Dog Care Manual.* Barron's Educational Series, Inc., Hauppauge, New York, 1986.
Baer, Ted. *Communicating with Your Dog.* Barron's Educational Series, Inc., Hauppauge, New York, 1989.
——. *How to Teach Your Old Dog New Tricks.* Barron's Educational Series, Inc., Hauppauge, New York, 1991.

Useful Addresses and Literature

Frye, Fredric. *First Aid For Your Dog*. Barron's Educational Series, Inc., Hauppauge, New York, 1987.

Klever, Ulrich. *The Complete Book of Dog Care*. Barron's Educational Series, Inc., Hauppauge, New York, 1989.

———. *Dogs: A Mini Fact Finder*. Barron's Educational Series, Inc., Hauppauge, New York, 1990.

Pinney, Chris C. *Guide to Home Pet Grooming*. Barron's Educational Series, Inc., Hauppauge, New York, 1990.

Ullmann, Hans. *The New Dog Handbook*. Barron's Educational Series, Hauppauge, New York, 1984.

Vanacore, Connie and E. Irving Eldredge. *The New Complete Irish Setter*. Howell House, Inc., New York, New York, 1983.

Index

Index

Index

BARRON'S PET REFERENCE BOOKS

Barron's Pet Reference Books are and have long been the choice of experts and discerning pet owners. Why? Here are just a few reasons. These indispensable volumes are packed with 35 to 200 stunning full-color photos. Each provides the very latest expert information and answers questions that pet owners often wonder about.

BARRON'S PET REFERENCE BOOKS ARE:

AQUARIUM FISH (1350-6)
AQUARIUM FISH BREEDING (4474-6)
THE AQUARIUM FISH SURVIVAL MANUAL (9391-7)
AQUARIUM PLANTS MANUAL (1687-4)
BEFORE YOU BUY THAT KITTEN (1336-0)
BEFORE YOU BUY THAT PUPPY (1750-1)
THE BEST PET NAME BOOK EVER (4258-1)
CARING FOR YOUR SICK CAT (1726-9)
THE COMPLETE BOOK OF BUDGERIGARS (6059-8)
CARING FOR YOUR OLDER CAT (9148-5)
CARING FOR YOUR OLDER DOG (9149-3)
CARING FOR YOUR SICK CAT (1726-9)
THE CAT CARE MANUAL (1767-6)
CIVILIZING YOUR PUPPY (4953-5)
COMMUNICATING WITH YOUR DOG (4203-4)
THE COMPLETE BOOK OF CAT CARE (4613-7)
THE COMPLETE BOOK OF DOG CARE (4158-5)
THE COMPLETE BOOK OF PARAKEET CARE (1688-2)
THE DOG CARE MANUAL (9163-9)

FEEDING YOUR PET BIRD (1521-5)
GOLDFISH AND ORNAMENTAL CARP (9286-4)
GUIDE TO A WELL-BEHAVED CAT (1476-6)
GUIDE TO A WELL-BEHAVED PARROT (4996-9)
GUIDE TO HOME PET GROOMING (4298-0)
HEALTHY CAT, HAPPY CAT (9136-1)
HEALTHY DOG, HAPPY DOG (1842-7)
HOP TO IT: A Guide To Training Your Pet Rabbit (4551-3)
THE HORSE CARE MANUAL (1133-3)
HOW TO TEACH YOUR OLD DOG NEW TRICKS (4544-0)
INDOOR CATS (9449-2)
LABYRINTH FISH (5635-3)
NONVENOMOUS SNAKES (5632-9)
TROPICAL MARINE FISH SURVIVAL MANUAL (9372-0)
SECRET LIFE OF CATS, THE (6513-1)

Barron's Educational Series, Inc., 250 Wireless Boulevard, Hauppauge, New York 11788. For sales information call toll-free: 1-800-645-3476.

In Canada: Georgetown Book Warehouse, 34 Armstrong Avenue, Georgetown, Ontario L7G 4R9. Call toll-free: 1-800-247-7160.

Order from your favorite bookstore or pet shop.   ISBN Prefix 0-8120

(#64) R 3/96

Perfect for Pet Owners!